An Arab Pastor Living Under
Persecution in the Holy Land

IN THE
BACKYARD
OF JESUS

STEVEN N. KHOURY

Living Sacrifice Book Company
Bartlesville, OK 74005

In the Backyard of Jesus

Living Sacrifice Book Company
P.O. Box 2273
Bartlesville, OK 74005-2273

Originally published as *Diplomatic Christianity*, © 2008, HMC Press, Jerusalem, Israel.

ISBN 978-0-88264-054-9

Edited by Lynn Copeland

Design and production by Genesis Group

Printed in the United States of America

Unless otherwise indicated, Scripture references are from the *New King James* version, © 1979, 1980, 1982 by Thomas Nelson Inc., Publishers, Nashville, Tennessee.

For author interviews, please contact
Calvary Jerusalem Ministries at (0119) 722-54-460-3337.

Visit our website for more info:
www.holylandmissions.org

To my father
for living out what he believes.
His faithful dedication and perseverance
in his calling have affected my life,
resulting in who I am today.

Contents

Acknowledgments

I want to thank:

Jesus Christ: for giving His life on the cross so that I may have eternal life.

My mom and dad: for teaching me to appreciate family, ministry, and the calling.

My beautiful wife, Shari: for faithfully leaving her homeland to come serve with me, and for her amazing creativity.

Paul, Peter, and Lydia: for encouraging me to follow my heart's calling. I thank God for their faithfulness to the Lord's ministry.

Michael & Cheryl Leigh: for trusting in the Lord, support on this project, and their continual support of my cause.

Blake & Mary Everman: for their friendship and their commitment to reaching the Middle East, and time spent on this project.

F. P. and Kim: for believing in my message and for their unique creativity with this book.

Partners: for anyone who has ever blessed our cause with support, financially or spiritually, and for standing behind us as we face the front-lines.

The Voice of the Martyrs (VOM): for their love and support for the persecuted church. My heart cannot express enough how thankful I am to VOM. I call you all our big brother, every single one at VOM, from Jim Dau all the way down to the person who turns the lights on and off at your headquarters. Your willingness to voice our voices, and your sacrifice to carry our cries is inspiring. You are all my heroes, and I thank the Lord Almighty for you all, and I ask Him every day to bless you and enlarge your territory!

Dear friend and co-laborer in ministry,

I pray that the story of my life may inspire you to stand up and face confrontation with the non-negotiable truths that Jesus Christ has given to us in His Word. This generation of Christians has the ability to unite and accomplish great things.

I invite you to visit our growing ministry in Jerusalem and to view my website for additional support (www.holylandmissions.org).

Pastor Steven Khoury

Foreword

I FIRST MET Steven Khoury at our regional conference in June 2008. He had been invited to speak about the situation faced by Christians in the West Bank and Israel. I was impressed with this unusual young Arab, who was nothing like the angry Palestinian stereotype. He was easy to talk to, personable, and passionate about his calling. Both Steven and his wife, Shari, were committed to serving their neighbors in the West Bank in any way they could from their home in Bethlehem, reaching those no Western missionary could ever touch.

I was impressed with the man when I met him, but my regard for Steven only grew throughout the week as I heard him speak. That Sunday morning, he led us in a communion service that celebrated the promise of future redemption through Christ's sacrifice along with the reality of suffering while we are here on earth.

Today, The Voice of the Martyrs is proud to be one of Steven's partners in ministry. For several years now, we have sponsored a Christmas celebration for the poor believers and seekers in the Khourys' West Bank neighborhood, where attendees receive blankets and other needed items while hearing about a Man who died for them.

My wife, Peggy, was privileged to spend several days with Steven in Israel last year. Steven wanted Peggy to be able to meet the believers that he works with, so they met with several families in their homes for coffee. One of the people she met was a carpenter who had been rejected by his family after he trusted Christ. Even so, Peggy said this carpenter had a deep love for the Lord.

Steven has consistently demonstrated his love for the Palestinian people and their Jewish neighbors, while refusing to compromise on the message of Christ that he shares. He has traveled relentlessly in the past four years in cooperation with VOM, raising awareness and calling for action on behalf of persecuted believers in Israel, the West Bank, and Gaza. He has led Bible studies all over the Holy Land with former Muslims, the children of high-level extremist group leaders, and Messianic Jews.

He planted a church in a city of which another pastor had said church planting is possible "anywhere but there." That city has produced more suicide bombers than any other in Palestine. My wife visited a church service in that city. No one was willing to rent to the church, so the church met in a private home. That day, Steven preached a powerful message on the poor man Lazarus and the rich man, and several people gave their lives to Christ. The fact that he would even choose to preach in that city spoke of his fearless determination to share the gospel anywhere, without reservation.

Steven is no stranger to opposition to his message, having borne his share of verbal and physical assaults and threats. But Steven's faith overcomes all forms of opposition as he ministers in this land torn between so many. His commitment to the message is why VOM is proud to work with him, and so proud to be a link in the chain through Steven reaching many for Christ in the Holy Land.

JIM DAU
President, The Voice of the Martyrs–USA

Introduction

RELIGIOUS CONFRONTATION is one of Satan's favorite tactics. The Christians of the world are being challenged with the argument that they must accept others' opinions and respect them as their own. You must not only tolerate but accept others' lifestyle choices. You mustn't call people out about what they believe; this is selfish and narrow-minded. You must not confront others about the truths of life as they present their own spins on reality. Christians are falling for these philosophies left and right. We are backing down from speaking God's truth for fear of alienation and persecution. Still, there are those who defy Satan as they try to awaken Christendom to the realities they must face.

We have already won the battle through the work of our beloved Savior Jesus Christ. The confrontations and persecutions in our lives are pulled straight from Satan's bag of tricks. Read this book in conjunction with Daniel 3 and focus your mind on how persecution can revive an entire nation for Christ. Learn how to face confrontation with the Word of God and Christ's simple message of grace.

I hope that you will not be offended if I ask God to touch your life. I pray He gives you the strength, wisdom, and joy He has promised.

> Dear Lord, I pray for my readers and ask that you would give them strength to stand up for their faith, wisdom from Your Word, and insight into the blessings that come from being true to Your cross. Lord, we are Your children. Do with us as You wish, and we ask that You go before us preparing our way daily to meet You one day soon. In Jesus' name I pray. Amen.

I have been crucified with Christ; it is no longer
I who live, but Christ lives in me; and the life which I
now live in the flesh I live by faith in the Son of God,
who loved me and gave Himself for me.

GALATIANS 2:20

Courage is not simply one of the virtues,
but the form of every virtue at the testing point.

C. S. LEWIS

CHAPTER 1

My Life

Growing Up in the Land of Christ

DO YOU SOMETIMES shun people and situations, feeling that everyone hates you, as if being a Christian makes you an enemy to everyone else? Many Christians are uncomfortable with the prospect of confrontation, of being challenged about their faith. It is so much easier to just keep silent among peers than to speak out and risk being rejected. I find that confrontation is like a disease: it's something everyone hopes to avoid, and when it occurs it weakens people. At times, it tends to alienate outspoken believers from everyone else.

Growing up in the city where Jesus of Nazareth was born has not always brought me acceptance. People all over the world call my home the Holy Land, a place of simple purity and light. Few realize the deep struggles, persecutions, and confrontations that Christians here face on a daily basis—living in the midst of conflict between Muslims and Jews, Israel and the Palestinian territories.

Confrontation and persecution were some of the first realities I awoke to growing up in the Holy Land. I will never forget those shocking moments in my life that put me face to face with danger. I was forced to encounter the harsh realities of what I believe beginning when I was eight years old. These realities helped prepare me for the tough times that my family and I currently face. But if not for the tough times that help us wrestle with what we believe, how will we know that God is real and that Jesus is right there beside us?

On many occasions I hid under my bed holding my Bible close to my heart, hugging it like a small child hugs his mama's neck, crying and shaking at every noise I heard outside my windows—constantly wondering whether it would be an enraged person threatening our living compound, a single sniper's gunshot, or hundreds of bullets flying at our home. Close encounters with death haunt me every day, keeping me in touch with the reality that without Christ my battle is already lost.

O Little Town of Bethlehem

I was born to an Arab Palestinian Christian family in the city of Jerusalem and I grew up in the town of Bethlehem. Bethlehem is famous for being the birthplace of Jesus Christ. As we all know, it is a unique town, with much history associated with it. Its people, both Jews and Arabs, have a long history in the region with distinctive cultural elements, such as a beautiful two-week-long wedding tradition and a hospitable, family-based society. It is also a region filled with religious and political unrest and potential conflict in daily social interactions.

On a typical morning you can go out on the streets and watch the storeowners and employees open up their shops at 9 a.m. The sun's blazing heat starts to take effect on the streets. You'll see people racing to take a taxi to work, school children walking or bicycling to school, and shepherds riding donkeys with sheep following behind, trying to find the green spots on the hillside to get their share of food.

I remember when I was ten years old, grocery shopping with my father would take hours. This is because large superstores like Wal-Mart don't take very well to the West Bank, so we would have to go to separate stores for every single type of item we needed. They were our mini Wal-Marts, if I may. I was never too particularly excited to visit the live chicken store, which sold solely and quite obviously, live chickens. This was a separate store from the meat store, which we would have to go down another block to find.

> *Close encounters with death haunt me every day, keeping me in touch with the reality that without Christ my battle is already lost.*

When I was old enough to go by myself, I would order 2 kilos of chicken from the man wearing a white smock. The more pounds my mother ordered me to get, the heavier the burden became and the more I dreaded it because, in my culture, the young boys are taught to be tough and strong. Only the strong survive, boy! Do not cry! Suck it up till the end! I remember being taught that a real man is made to stand strong, never with his head tilted down. The storeowner would take a live chicken from the coop and place it into a machine. When the machine closed, it cleaned and steamed the chicken. The awful sounds the chicken made as it died would ring loudly in my ears, but I could not falter; I had a mission. I was to bring the cleaned chicken home for my mother to cook. Then I could do as I wished until I was needed again.

Entertainment as the typical Westerner knows it is not really offered in my town. We create our own entertainment, often depending on elements like what street we live on or how many buildings surround our house. For fun my friends and I would create a different game every week. Some days we would wad up newspapers to play soccer with or throw rocks at the Israeli soldiers we saw.

Since we live in a family-based culture, every weekend we would visit with one of my father's nine uncles. This typically entailed eating eight meals all throughout the day, laughing, playing, and occasionally picking on the unfamiliar kids in our many uncles' more foreign neighborhoods. Bicycles were a big thing in the neighborhood. Each kid would do something different with his bike to show it off. The girls, on the other hand, would diligently work to learn from their mom or older sisters how to cook and clean by the age of twelve. Adults would sit and play chess, one of the many popular Middle Eastern games, or sit smoking the "Hubbly Bubbly" (a traditional Middle Eastern tobacco pipe, or *hookah*) on the side of the street.

School in the 1980s was a very interesting time for me and the others around me. Out of the nine months of school we were supposed to attend, I would go only about five months spread throughout the year. I had to change schools several times starting from kindergarten all the way up to high school. My formative years were spent growing up in the time of *Intifada*, an act of resistance by the Palestinians against the presence of Israel in the Palestinian territories. All of our men, from twelve-year-old boys to their forty-year-old fathers, were urged to riot and demonstrate daily against the presence of the Israeli military. This was a clear message that Israel was not welcome in Palestinian towns.

My day would start at about 6 a.m. standing out in the cold in line at the checkpoint, waiting to be searched by security to cross from Bethlehem into East Jerusalem where my school was located. Soldiers would empty my backpack, pat me down, and sometimes lift my shirt to make sure I had no weapons. Everyone had to face the same humiliating checking, regardless of age, gender, or political stance. In the end, only our nationality mattered—the fact that we were Palestinians made us suspect. Geographically, getting to Jerusalem should usually be a mere thirty-minute walk from my home, but due to everyday tensions it wound up taking a two-hour ride in a car. These daily checkpoints made my school experience significantly more difficult. Think of the security agents you typically see at an airport. Then multiply that by ten. Now, for the Transportation Security Administration (TSA) agent in the airport it is just a job, but these checkpoint guards not only viewed it as an occupation, they seemed to take pleasure in searching us, at times stripping us, and humiliating us. Occasionally they beat us just because we laughed in line or gave them the wrong look or attitude. Despite this, I did like the soldiers for one reason. As young kids, we were often sent back home two or three times a week from school, as if that were a horrible punishment.

Then, when we did make it to school, especially at my second school in Bethlehem, we would sometimes be sent home for weeks because the older boys would throw rocks and Molotov cocktails at the soldiers speeding by our school street. When that would happen we would be gassed out of our rooms and lined up against the walls for a couple of hours as the soldiers checked our bodies from head to toe. Then, once they were satisfied that we all were weapon- and bomb-free, we'd be sent home.

This was part of the daily life for young students and teachers during the school year. Aside from that, we had all the usual drama of a typical Western school. I, like many others my age, experienced the temptations of such things as girls, but thankfully drugs and many other addictive habits were not yet widely introduced in our society. To talk to a girl we usually had to use discreet sign language. This was because, in such a small community with such strong cultural views, you could end up cashing in your singles-life card by having your family decide you two should be married right away.

Dating to us is an official engagement, holding hands is a serious phase-two engagement, and kissing, well, first hit the altar, then kiss all you want. Of course, there were the occasional lovebirds who were untraditional and had their share of drama and romance. But usually the boy would end up getting beaten by his father for holding hands and the girl would get grounded and punished, depending on the level of disgrace she brought, or was perceived to bring, upon the family.

I am often asked how people survive and put food on the table in a society filled with wars and unrest. Since employment is uncertain, you learn to make the little go a long way, until the next opportunity comes to put food on the table. You could get a job for one day and not the next. You could find a grocery store open one day and closed the following day. Out of ten families it is not unusual to find six of them unemployed. This atmosphere creates a sense of desperation to find food and clothing at almost any cost. It wasn't uncommon for my brothers and I, like many others, to pass down toys and clothes from eldest to youngest; even if the items were broken or stained, we learned to enjoy them.

Train Up a Child in the Way He Should Go

Thankfully, I grew up in a Christian home. In fact, my father is a pastor and a missionary. He was raised in the Greek Orthodox church. Nine of his uncles and three of his cousins were all Greek Orthodox priests, so since childhood he had prepared and trained to enter priesthood. In Arabic, our last name, Khoury, translates to "priest." Our original roots go back to the Island of Crete, so some would call us Greek Arabs. Most of the Palestinian Arabs today are Muslims, while approximately 1.5% of Palestinians living in the Holy Land are Christians.

Persecution Continues
Where It Began

ISRAEL IS KNOWN as the Holy Land, the place where Jesus was born, died, and rose again. But just as Jesus was persecuted, so are Christians living in modern-day Israel—Christians like Salvator. Salvator is a Palestinian Arab Christian living in the midst of hostility.

"I am an evangelist to Muslims in this area," Salvator says. "Whenever I would go to a Muslim village I would take Christian literature, DVDs, and other evangelism tools to help Muslims understand Christ. Each time I would return to my car to leave, I would find windows broken, tires slashed, and once the lug nuts on my tires were loosened so that the tires fell off shortly after I drove away.

"I would often find death threats written to me. One said, 'You will be dying soon. *Allahu Akbar*' [God is great]. Sometimes they smashed my windows and put them in my car, they left notes at my home, and even left a death threat in my post office box.

"I was frightened for my wife and children but I just held on to God. When God spoke to me He was confirming to me that there was a reason why He put me in these areas and He is with me and will not leave. Whatever happens . . . I go to minister and do God's will for the salvation of souls. Whatever happens to me, even if I die, I know that I, my wife, and my children are in the hands of God."

Both of my parents came from traditional Christian Arab homes, born in Jerusalem and entrenched in an Arab society.

At age seventeen my father stumbled upon a little church in the streets of Jerusalem where he could hear an evangelist preaching, and decided to go inside to listen. He heard the gospel message of salvation and what it was to be born again. He heard a story of heaven and hell and God's promises for His children. This message of salvation by grace through the blood of Christ was a foreign teaching to him; he had been taught all his life that it took the actions of many—the Orthodox church, your daily works, the saints, and Jesus—to get into heaven. My father couldn't contain the joy he found in these new promises, so he jumped up, charging toward the front and asking how he could receive Jesus. His life was changed forever.

When he first became a believer and professed that a man named Jesus Christ changed his life, he was made out to be a traitor or a spy working for the IDF (Israel Defense Forces) or the CIA. By deciding to become "born again," which was commonly thought to be a Western term, he betrayed his family, culture, and traditional church.

Several years later, as my father knelt praying at the Garden Tomb, he met a gentleman from the far-off country of the United States of America. Though they could not communicate directly, my father used an interpreter to find out more about this man. As they spoke, the American asked why my father, a local traditional Orthodox Christian, would be praying here in the Garden Tomb. He began to inquire what was so important to my father, asking if perhaps he could pray with him. My father happily shared his testimony and added how his heart felt heavy with a burden for ministry to his people in the land. But the problem was that he did not know how to preach and teach the Bible.

"So you're asking God to open a door for you to get your Bible degree?" the man asked.

"I do not know a place to go to or where to start," my father said, "but I know God's message must be heard."

The man smiled and said, "Well, I think your prayers have been answered. See, I'm the president of a Bible college back home in the United States. Pack your bags," he said, "and come back to the school with me."

And so the journey began for my father to attend Bible college. Two years later when he returned to Jerusalem for the summer, he met my mother, Elvira. She then went back to the U.S. with him where they both completed different degrees at the Bible college. They attended four years in Springfield, Missouri, learning and studying, growing closer and closer to God. When they graduated and returned to Israel, they started a ministry in Bethlehem and called it First Baptist Church of Bethlehem.

For us, it was the second miracle birth after the birth of Jesus. My father and mother began the Bethlehem church in a small two-bedroom apartment. However, the tiny congregation was soon kicked out because of the noise, overcrowding, and lack of decent parking. My parents immediately began praying for land and a building of their own. With the help and prayers of strong believers, and through months of hard saving and planning, one year later they got enough money to pay a contractor to build a new building for their people.

Due to the limited size of the land, they decided to attach a house to the church. This house became my family's home. Therefore every activity, meeting, event, problem, and persecution that was aimed directly at the church affected us first. Sometimes this would affect me negatively as a child and I would try to weasel out of my church responsibilities by feigning sickness. My parents never said anything. They seemed to know that, as I lay in bed in the quiet house with nothing to do, I would begin to feel horribly guilty. As the songs and my father's preaching wafted through the windows I would feel even worse. From then on, when I began feeling lazy or irresponsible I would remind myself that it was better to be in church, even if I lacked the will that particular day, than to feel guilty as I heard the praise and worship music I was missing permeate our walls.

When I was sixteen years old, the Lord finally got a hold of my heart. Until that point I had sort of skimmed through life. I had a heart and love for Jesus, but didn't fully understand God's work in my life or the lives of my family. It was hard growing up as a child not knowing why these things, these persecutions, seemed to always come our way. My childhood was ripped away from me by persecution after persecution. There is a saying in Arabic: "If only the walls could speak, they bear many secrets and scars."

It wasn't until age sixteen that I woke up to what I had been missing. I then realized that God wanted to use my life to make a difference, that I was called to full-time ministry. And though the world around me would have me believe I was nothing and would never amount to anything, my parents prayed and worked in my life to show me a different way.

Face to Face with My Faith

In 1996, I went with my sister and cousin to the Olympics in Atlanta, Georgia. We went into the streets to pass out tracts and talk about our lives, hoping that we would make a difference. Being the more outgoing one of the group, I went into every street in downtown Atlanta witnessing, telling people to believe in Jesus, and explaining to them how He changed my life. By the third day I had passed out about 3,000 tracts and talked to as many as 200 people.

One day as I wandered around I found myself walking down a street with beautiful drawings and art etched on the walls. I now know that this art is called graffiti and the more you see the more likely you are to be in a dangerous part of town. At the time, however, all I could think of was how there was no art on the streets of my town, and how, compared to ours, these streets were colorful, artsy, and creative. After awhile I noticed other things, like the smells, the larger shadowy places, and the difference in mannerisms here than in the other parts of town.

It wasn't until age sixteen that I woke up to what I had been missing. I then realized that God wanted to use my life to make a difference, that I was called to full-time ministry.

As I talked to people I also noticed the new accents and strange looks the people gave me. As I knelt down to pick up a few more tracts I had in my bag, I saw a man's foot come out of nowhere, and as I got up he backed me into a corner. I felt something sharp by my neck. Unlike most foreigners in America, however, this did not faze me as the man hoped it would. I am from an area where I felt confrontation, physical and spiritual, every second of the day.

I told him Jesus loved him. He said he knew that; "Now give me your money." I asked him if he believed, but he stepped closer, pushing me harder and harder against the wall. This time he motioned with another sharp object in his jacket pocket. There was a second of silence between this man and myself. In this silence, as I stared face to face with a mad man, Satan began attacking my mind. He repeated the words of our neighbors: *You are worthless, a loser, always doing the wrong thing at the wrong time. You think you're doing things for God? Well, look at where He's gotten you.*

Suddenly, we heard a loud boom just around the block. It was the terrorist bomb that went off that day (July 27) at the Centennial Olympic Park, which happened to be the exact location I was headed for. This thug had saved my life! God hadn't forgotten me! God had saved me from the atrocities of man. Immediately my aggressor lost the will to challenge me. He was so afraid he almost cried. Bombs, however, do not scare me much, as they are part of my everyday life. This experience gave me a unique opportunity to witness to this man. I wound up giving him my money anyway, because the Lord loves a cheerful giver and it seemed like he truly needed it. I got the chance to pray with him. I was happy. Spiritually I was alive and awakened once again. When I went back to my hometown, I decided to make up my sixteen years of simply surviving in Bethlehem and start making a bigger difference in the lives of people around me for as long as God kept me on earth.

Every material possession we work for will stay behind; it is only the lives we affect that will matter in heaven.

Time to Let Go and Live

In the summer of 2000, at age eighteen, I left Bethlehem to study at the same school that my father graduated from in Springfield, Missouri. It was the first time I ever said good-bye to my parents, knowing that for the next several years, which is a long time for a village boy, my home would be somewhere else. The relationship my family and I share is a life sealed with blood spilled from political and religious unrest. I will share in later chapters some of the stories that manifest the unique relationship we have as a family. But before I end this chapter of my life I want to encourage you to enjoy life while you have it. Life is too short to live carrying a big load. I like to say, *"Let go and let live."*

Listen to me when I say to expect the unexpected, live life to the fullest loving God as your Savior, loving others as worthy human beings, and loving yourself because you matter to God. Nothing is impossible with Him. Keep holding on to what you know best. Jesus loves you. Do not back down. Do not give in to the pressures of the world around you. You are a walking testimony to God's love and grace.

I see many people, some friends and family, living and breathing in the afternoon, and by evening I see their names and faces in the tragic death lists on the five o'clock news. I always like to remind myself to keep smiling because we aren't taking anything with us to heaven. Every material possession we work for will stay behind; it is only the lives we affect that will matter in heaven. Remind yourself to smile and be confident in who God made you. You and I mean the world to Him; this is something that you take to your deathbed. So in the next chapter I would like to invite you to take a closer look into the life of a Christian living in the Middle East. Fighting a victorious spiritual war and keeping the gospel message real and alive among the Arab and Jewish nations is my passion in life. Please keep your hearts and minds open as you read these stories and remember to always: *"Expect the unexpected to happen in your life."*

Character is what a man is in the dark.

DWIGHT L. MOODY

The whole problem with the world is that fools
and fanatics are always so certain of themselves,
but wiser people so full of doubts.

BERTRAND RUSSELL

CHAPTER 2

Let's Get Real

Persecution on My Front Doorstep

DID YOU KNOW many of the things that happen in the West also happen in the Middle East when it comes to political correctness and sharing our faith? Persecution can occur at work, at a favorite coffee shop, at the bookstore, at school, at the gym, even in our own households. Persecution and confrontation are all around us. Usually when this happens we tend to act like ostriches, burying our heads deep in the ground, waiting until the all-clear is sounded. We play games with ourselves and say it is okay to agree with others' positions as long as we don't get hurt or make enemies. The problem is that we are spiritually already behind enemy lines. Satan's army is upon us already, and the sooner we accept this, the faster we will overcome it. *"The first solution to any problem is admitting there is one."*

I remember visiting a coffee shop not too long ago to find a quiet solace in which to focus on my writing. I tried to find the smallest table in the furthest corner so I could concentrate and be away from everyone. Middle Easterners are just naturally loud sometimes and I tend to get easily distracted. My chance of finding a small table was slim, so I chose a round table that had a few empty seats. As I began to read and write, a gentleman came and sat at my table, right across from me. He began talking to the girl sitting next to me. I paid no attention to them as I tried desperately to focus. Soon enough the girl got up and left, and a few minutes later I found myself begrudgingly entering into a conversation with the talkative man. I thought maybe if I continued writing and shaking my head he'd leave me alone. Instead he began talking about life's problems, his personal issues, and the wars.

It dawned on me then through his body language that he was a Christian trying to find common ground to share with me about Jesus Christ. After about twenty minutes of him passionately talking and me shaking my head, I looked him straight in the eyes and said, "Would you just come out and tell me already that Jesus Christ died on the cross for my sins, and that He can give me eternal life to spend with Him if I repent and trust in Him?"

He looked at me and said, "Man, you're a Christian! You should have told me."

"So should've you," I countered, "about twenty minutes ago." I told him it is a simple message from a simple origin. This man had meant well and had been courageous to attempt to share the gospel with strangers, but I felt that he was trained to be too timid in his diplomacy in what he says and how he acts. It was as if he was being held back by trying to avoid confrontation or being singled out.

I did not continue talking about the subject since the poor man had had it bad enough already. I told him that Jesus loved him and that He has already done the work for us. All we have to do is tell others about it and keep it simple. The message is real and self-sufficient. He looked at me with tears in his eyes and said that what I had told him had uplifted him and that he was glad God had given us this chance to talk.

Reaching the Lost at Any Cost

As a Palestinian Christian, and now a pastor, I am a representative of a side of the conflict many people never see. My life shows the harsh realities my people face. Hopefully my testimony will be used to further knowledge of the tremendous need of the Palestinian people and the nucleus of Christians in my region.

So why would I return to Israel, choosing to live in the Palestinian territories when many people there are anxious to leave and live in the West? When I came back from college and returned to Bethlehem, I had only one thing on my mind: to make restitution for all the years I had lost existing in Israel and not doing enough for the gospel's sake. I knew there was so much to be done among the 7.8 million people living here in this country. The task seemed daunting, but I found strength in my family's love and God's direction.

For the first several months I spent my time fasting and praying, asking God what I should do and where I should go, seeking an answer, a vision, or a new path. But persecution doesn't just make you afraid, it also makes you resentful. For a while I struggled with staying in Israel. After all, this is a hard field. The people my father tried to help would as often as not betray his love and commitment after he spent so much time, love, care, and even money on them. Why should I help them? Many would even come, crying crocodile tears and weeping for salvation to get us to bring them into our church and home, with the dark motives of causing a public confrontation or scandal, trying to shame us and our Savior's name. My heart was heavy mourning all the martyrs and fallen comrades in the faith who were killed, beaten, and betrayed by family, friends, and enemies for professing their loyalty to the Messiah, Jesus Christ.

However, I came to realize that there is persecution everywhere, for everyone. How could I leave the people I was called to minister to just because there would be certain costs? Didn't I have an advantage, having grown up in this region, already knowing what the costs might be?

Persecution on My Doorstep

I remember once when I was only twelve years of age and my father had been out on visitation passing out food to people in need. He had just called to tell me that he would return in about ten minutes because there was some shooting outside our church compound and he wanted to make sure we were all okay. I remember asking him to be careful driving and to turn off the headlights and switch the console lights on. When the doorbell finally rang, I thought it was my father needing my help carrying in leftover food from his car. A small alarm went off in my mind, though, when I remembered that he usually called before he drove down the hill that led to our garage. I noticed that the electricity was out in the neighborhood and our whole street was pitch black. I did not hear the sound of the car, only the long howls of stray dogs roaming the streets at night. The only thing that seemed to be working was our old battery-run doorbell at the compound gate.

I peeked out through the upstairs window and saw four men wearing traditional red scarves (also known as *keffiyeh*) of Palestinian resistance fighters. I knew they wore these scarves only when prepared to fight to the death. The men covered their faces, their dark eyes still a sober image. All I could think of was my father—they wanted my father, and this confrontation was meant to be life or death for him. I remember kneeling down right by the window and praying, "Lord, hold my father and release me, please."

Suddenly I knew what I must do. I got off my knees, walked to our home's front door, and opened it. Then I went to the second door to the front of our building. Even though my mind seemed to resist, my body kept going toward the court-yard door, the final door between the dangerous men and me. This door has a red button on the inside that you press to open the gate door. As I put my finger on the red button, I kept thinking that I was just a young man, but my father needed to live because he could still do a lot more for the gospel's sake. There were still many lives that needed to be changed and reached. It was clear to me: he would live and I would not. So I pressed the red button and pulled the large metal door toward me and stepped out, closing it behind me so they couldn't get to my younger brothers or sister.

"Who do you want?" I asked.

"Steven," they said boldly, "is your father here?"

My eyes couldn't help wandering down to the guns in their front pockets or the dried blood covering the knives dangling close by, evidence of an earlier hit. With a loud voice stronger than I felt I told them my father was not here and I hoped he did not come home. The four men stepped closer to me. "Where is your father?"

Silently I thanked God for the strength He was giving me and asked Him again to take me and spare my father.

"Why do you want to hurt him?" I asked the masked men. "What harm has he done to you?" The men let me talk. I asked them to tell me what message they had for him, that I'd make sure he got it.

Silently I thanked God for the strength He was giving me and asked Him again to take me and spare my father. I stood my ground, waiting for the men to attack, to kill me there. Suddenly, whether from shame of killing a helpless kid or some other unknown force, they backed up from the gate and ran back out into the night.

I decided to stay outside just in case they came back again or my father came home while they were watching. Even though it was cold, and I was barefoot with only shorts and a shirt on, I wanted to stay until my father drove down the hill safely. After about thirty minutes of squatting by the corner of the front gate, trying to keep warm, I saw a large cloud of billowing smoke rolling down the hill: it was my father. The water hose on his car had popped just a quarter of a mile down the street. God's angels had worked in mysterious ways, always protecting His children, reminding me that He is always there.

The Forgotten People

Yes, persecution is everywhere for everyone. It is at your very doorstep. No matter where you are, the power of Satan grows stronger every sunrise and every sundown. There are millions and millions of persecuted people throughout the world. If every missionary wrote a hundred books apiece we could still never even glimpse the tip of persecution's iceberg. It is the Palestinian people, however, who have been placed on my heart today. Therefore it will be the persecution of the Palestinian people that I will try to share with you now. According to recent statistics there are approximately 1.5 million Palestinian people in all of Israel, the West Bank, and the Gaza Strip combined. Growing anger and hatred from the hearts of the Palestinians toward Israel is very evident. Often children as young as five are trained to be hateful, angry, and jealous of the Jewish people. Conversations heard on the streets frequently include statements like, "Israel took my father's land," or "Israel shot

If every missionary wrote a hundred books apiece we could still never even glimpse the tip of persecution's iceberg.

so-and-so." They talk about the number of deaths from recent Israeli attacks and the details of the people involved in that day's death toll.

I cannot deny that many innocent Palestinian women and children have died at the hands of the Israeli army. Most of the anger of our youngest generations is simply the consequence of the reality that they are being fed hatred fueled by the hidden motives of the people in charge. Misleading and wrong information is propagated into the young minds of the Palestinian people, often portrayed through "facts" or the opinions of the media.

It is not the Arab traditions that ruin the younger generations. The Palestinians' mentality is that these lands are theirs, and they should keep them. Their culture dictates a strong respect for elders, something that the rest of the world seems to be lacking as of late. Your word is still your bond and the basis of honor and pride, and keeping your promises is still greatly valued. Men should fight for their land and provide for their household, no matter the personal cost. I find this to be the general consensus of most American people regarding their own lands and families as well, and there is nothing wrong with any of this, as long as everyone around you holds to its integrity.

Despite this early training to despise the Jews, many Palestinians have come to wonder, "Where do we belong? Is Israel really our enemy? What will our future hold?" Others, like me, are slowly seeing the mentality of the Palestinian people shift. Many are willing to accept the Jews as neighbors, more than the radical freedom fighters would like to admit.

Even though I am a Palestinian Christian, I grew up having Jewish friends. I know that we are all living, breathing beings. While I don't think this is typical of most Israelis, in my experience some have the attitude that they do not care what happens or who gets killed, as long as there is no killing in their particular neighborhood.

Many people do not realize that eighty percent of the nation of Israel is secular, with lax moral values and dead spiritual lives. Most Jewish people do not follow the religion of Judaism. The Israelis like to say, "Live life hurting no one, live life to the fullest, and make money to enjoy what life offers."

Another point of difference is their mentality toward mandatory military service. Although almost every Israeli citizen has to serve in the military, I've never seen one young man or woman complain about it. In the minds of many of the young Israeli people, a Palestinian may or may not be a potential foe, but always assume he is an enemy. They always say that you can never know who to trust. Of course, this paranoia is largely supported by a realistic, constant fear of roadside bombings, rockets, and wired explosives strapped around the bodies of radical Palestinian freedom fighters. In the minds of the Israelis they won the war with Jehovah's help, thus it is their rightful land.

Contrary to many views held on the Middle Eastern conflicts, most Israelis would not mind living with Palestinian people as neighbors. Their mentality is "If we don't bother them, then they shouldn't bother us." You'd be surprised how many Israelis are upset about the building of the massive wall around the West Bank. They see it as inhumane and unfair.

Most of the tensions and racism in Israel are centralized around Jerusalem. Violence is a potential reality everywhere you go in Israel, but when you are the minority of the minorities—a Palestinian Christian like me—you are usually in a special category of deep, deep trouble, no matter how hard you try not to be.

I will never forget the day I was riding the school bus on my way home at about 2:30 in the afternoon. Right next to my school building was one of the largest bus stops outside the center of Jerusalem. It had been a target for many suicide bombers and car attacks against innocents waiting at the bus stop to go home. As we waited at the red light, I lay my head sleepily against the window. Suddenly I heard the squealing tires of a speeding car, driving on the opposite side of the road, careening toward the bus stop. It all happened so fast.

As the car approached the bus stop at top speed the man inside the car screamed, *"Allahu Akbar!"* ("God is great!"), waving his hands in the air. The undercover agents who typically patrol the stop shot bullets at the car, penetrating the windshield. As the car hit the curb and ran into the frightened crowd, bodies flew everywhere: to the other side of the road, on top of the nearby hill, even right by the tire of our school bus. All I could do was watch, registering forever in my mind the faces and bodies of all those innocent men, women, and children, just passing by, minding their own business.

Those bodies could have easily been any one of us on the bus or in my school that day. Time seemed to stop, then slowly tick-tock, tick-tock by as we all faced the reality and horror of the event that transpired right before our eyes. Tick-tock, tick tock. Is time running out for the people of the Holy Land?

Persecution for the Sake of the Cross

But car bombings weren't the only trouble we experienced. I passed many sleepless nights for fear of someone attacking my family, our house, or our church building. We were a target for the local radicals, whether Muslim or Jewish, because we were not afraid to speak up for the cross.

I remember sleeping with one foot in bed and the other on the floor, tossing and turning with my eyes half open, dozing off every few seconds, flinching at every sound or vibration in the darkness. Everywhere you go in Israel is a possible ground for confrontation. When you are an outspoken, born-again believer, you are always singled out for trouble.

Born-again Palestinians are usually alienated by everyone. Many of the Jews don't like us because we tell them their Messiah has already come, died, and rose again. Many Muslims don't like us because we teach that Jesus Christ is God and that He is the only way to heaven. And lastly, many of the Catholics don't like us because we tell their people that only Jesus' grace, not their works or their saints, can save them from their sins. These encounters are inevitable. In a city like Jerusalem, it is a simple fact that you could bump into a radical Muslim, Jew, or Catholic every single day.

Their message was delivered in a sickly calm voice: Stop preaching your message that Jesus is the Messiah and that He is the God-man sent from heaven as the way for salvation.

Daily threats were not uncommon during certain periods of my life. Radical extremists threatened us for our real and tangible faith. I remember one night waiting at the top of the hill leading to our garage for my father to pull up in the car. As he was coming up the hill he did not see the two men standing close to me, knives in their hands.

Just as my father pulled up right next to me he saw them. I will never forget the look he gave me right then—that look that said, "I love you, son. I am so sorry for all of this." He slowly turned the car off, got out, and asked the men to calm down. Their message was delivered in a sickly calm voice: Stop preaching your message that Jesus is the Messiah and that He is the God-man sent from heaven as the way for salvation. I remember these men telling my father that Mohammed is God's prophet and no other.

They raised the knife at us and waved it in our faces. It was a calm yet scary threat. They should have been at our throats, screaming. They should have been trying to fight, hand to hand, with my father. But somehow God had surrounded our driveway with an invisible cloud of peace.

My father looked at the sunken faces of these men and noticed that they looked hungry. I saw my father pull out some money from his pocket and give it to the two men. With the money in hand, they slowly turned, then ran away. What happened that night was something that I will cherish forever. Until then, I had never felt the true presence of God like that night. Right at that moment, I could promise you I heard multitudes singing and rejoicing in the empty church building behind us.

Since my father grew up not having an opportunity to get a Bible degree in the Holy Land, the Lord blessed him with several strong, Arabic-speaking, certified Bible college professors who came alongside him and helped him start a Bible college. Around that time we had a group of about nine young Muslim men attending our church services, two of whom were in our Bible college. That did not bode well with many Muslims in the community; it just gave them another excuse to target us. We turned no one down to sit in our services or to ask questions about Jesus, which only made them hate us more. It is very common for people of different faiths to turn away those wanting to attend a prayer meeting or seeking answers to their questions from the leaders of that religion.

Sameer, a handicapped man who traveled around in a manual wheelchair, was a new convert in our church around the time I was thirteen. When he heard why these radical aggressors threatened us, he decided to spend two weeks on the roof of our church, day and night, to watch over us. I wound up lovingly calling him "the handy handicapped man" because he came in very handy indeed. Since he had no sensation in his body he could not feel the cold. He stayed out all night on the church roof, overlooking the street. This is the most vulnerable spot on our building in threatening times. I thank God for brave men like Sameer. Today if you come to visit our church you would still see Sameer at the front of the church, singing and praising the Lord for saving him.

I was scared about eighty percent of the time when I was a kid, just walking down my own street, taking a local bus, or even playing with the neighborhood kids. I had the same fears I see behind the eyes of the Israelis; I never knew who my friends or enemies were or who truly liked or disliked me. But love always wins.

Late one night seven men repeatedly rang the doorbell and rapidly knocked on our front gate. The Israeli soldiers had been chasing them all night for throwing rocks at them. We heard some shooting in the street, then another frightened series of banging at the front gate. I looked up at my father and he told me to follow him outside. We walked out to the front gate and peeked out through the hole in the door. After standing there for a moment, looking out at whoever was at the gate, my father looked down at me, told me to back up and be strong, and then he pushed the red button and opened the gate.

The men wearing red and black masks were breathing hard and some were bleeding. They asked my father to let them in and protect them, to hide them until the Israeli soldiers left the area. My father was stuck between a rock and a hard place. If he said no, he would be aiding Israeli soldiers. If he said yes, he'd be putting himself and his family in danger and possibly aiding terror. He had to make a quick and diffi-

Keeping Watch on the Church in the Palestinian Territories

SAMEER HAS HAD a tough life. Born crippled, he had to walk on crude, homemade crutches, two sticks really, before finally getting a wheelchair. Just as he struggled with many surgeries and medical procedures on his legs, Sameer underwent a transformation on his soul. The fifty-three-year-old grew up in a Christian family but it wasn't until he began attending the Baptist church in Bethlehem, the only church of its kind in the Muslim-dominated West Bank, that he truly found Jesus.

But while knowing Jesus and going to church filled Sameer's heart with joy, he also encountered a new kind of suffering—the type of pain that comes with following Christ.

"Persecution at my church was regular during the *Intifada* [the assault Palestinians launched on Israelis for occupying what they claim is their land]. Muslims were coming into the community and they were angry," Sameer explained. "One Wednesday night, while we were just wrapping up the last song of praise and worship, our pastor was about to do his sermon when we heard shouting at the church's door. Muslims slammed through the doors of the church, screaming for us to stop worshiping, saying they didn't want us there, and hurling rocks. They rushed into the sanctuary with small, thin bats and began hitting the pastor and everyone gathered there. There were about fifty people. They hit me as I struggled to hold on to my crutches. They also busted into our Christian bookstore and began tearing out pages in the books and destroying everything.

(continued)

(continued)

"They did this many times. Many times they attacked the church. I began dragging myself up to the second floor of the church building, near the bell tower so I could be a lookout to keep watch and alert the security guards on the first floor if trouble was on the way. We had old-style walkie-talkies. I would stay up all night until 3 or 4 in the morning. It was exhausting but honestly, in this persecution, I felt joyful. I felt like I was giving something to the Lord. In the flesh I felt afraid but when you have faith in the Lord, nothing shakes or scares you!"

cult choice. My father looked at me and I knew what he was thinking. His face had that look of compassion and forgiveness that he gets when helping those in need. It was a look that asked, "How can I preach love and forgiveness if I have no compassion for my enemies?"

These guys were from one of the largest Palestinian refugee camps in the West Bank, right across the street from us, where most of the attacks aimed at us originated from. My father told them to hurry up and come in quickly. The shock showed through their eyes as we not only let them inside the safety of our compound, but took them up to the church sanctuary. They expected to be put in a dirty basement or garage. But no, my father knew that this was an opportunity to show them the love of Christ.

I went to get water, bread, and some other food for them from inside the house. As time passed, my father talked to them about how violence will get us nowhere, that the only answer is love and forgiveness, and that we must show mercy to others. I also remember my father taking advantage of the time and telling these young men that Jesus Christ died for their sins and will give them new life, freeing them from their extremist thinking, hatred, and anger. They were shocked that we loved them so much that we would bring them into our holy place, whereas when they are in their mosques, we Christians are not even allowed to step into the outside part, let alone the inside.

These men frightened me. I remember asking my father why we had to do this. I reminded him, as if he didn't understand, that these were the same people who persecuted us daily. Then my father told me something that would change my young life. He said, "Steven, the only thing these people know is killing and hatred. They expect us to hate them, too. But if we show them hatred we will betray Christ. Love and forgiveness is a choice that we must make to prove to them that our God is real."

> "If we show them hatred we will betray Christ. Love and forgiveness is a choice that we must make to prove to them that our God is real."

After I let my father's words sink in, I began immediately to go one by one, asking them what I could do for them as they were lying on the floor, catching their breath and wondering what would happen to them by the end of the night. When I came to the fourth man he looked me steadily in the eyes, breathing slowly now, perhaps because the shooting outside had finally stopped. "Steve," he said to me, "you are a brave man to face an angry group all alone at night. You are a good man." I realized then from his deep brown eyes and deep voice that he was one of the men who were planning on killing my father the night his car broke down. The next Sunday seven unmasked, mysterious men came into the sanctuary, sat in the back left corner and heard the gospel message. After the service all seven men shook my hand, then my father's hand, and left without a word, as if they felt the presence of God's love and passion in the acts they'd witnessed.

I'd like to ask you to let these thoughts work through in your mind as my heart and the heart of my people lies open before you. I have shared these small parts of my life to help you see a clearer picture of the reality of life in Israel and the West Bank territories. When you are asked about your faith or beliefs, do not be afraid to speak your heart or do the right thing. God is with you every step of the way. No matter where you are, He knows your weaknesses and He knows your needs. I want to ask you to internalize these stories you read. These are real parts of my past, present, and future, just as your daily life is real to you.

You and I as Christians are being pushed every day to the edge because we are not willing to be "politically correct" with what we believe. We are pressured in some shape or form to change what we believe.

Join us in realizing what's going on in the world around us. Get real with yourself because you and I as Christians are being pushed every day to the edge because we are not willing to be "politically correct" with what we believe. We are pressured in some shape or form to change what we believe and to accept the views of others by force or cunning.

First, you must accept your life and your own situational reality. Go ahead, climb over those walls in your spiritual life and get closer to Christ. My message and your message should be real and simple. Jesus Christ turned my life around. He gave me something that no one else could, and He can do the same for you if you trust Him and let Him work in your life.

With all the circumstances and consequences, I still thank God every day that He created me and put me in this area at this time in history. *"We are not only created with a purpose, we are created with the reality of victory."* So let's get real and begin testifying of Christ's simple message.

Where I was born and where and how I have lived
is unimportant. It is what I have done with where
I have been that should be of interest.

Dwight L. Moody

For I know the thoughts that I think toward you,
says the LORD, thoughts of peace and not of evil,
to give you a future and a hope.

Jeremiah 29:11

CHAPTER 3

Unexpected Love

Learning to Trust in God's Plan

WHEN I FLEW into Springfield, Missouri, to start Bible college, I could hardly put together a few sentences in English. I had never traveled by myself and I had only a little bit of money to buy a blanket, a pillow, and my personal hygiene products. I did not know how I would get to the college from the airport or even where I would sleep.

When I finally arrived at school I registered for my classes, got my books, and began preparing myself as best I knew how. I stuttered a lot, spoke broken English, and had a difficult-to-understand accent. At the time I did not know that I was walking in the shadow of a legend.

Trust God to Meet Your Needs

The first day of class I introduced myself as Steven Khoury and, before I could even attempt to get out where I was from, Professor Eli Haru exclaimed, "Khoury, as in Naim Khoury's son?" Now I was unsure of myself. "Yes," I said uncertainly. What did these people know of my father? Dr. Haru was an older man so as he slowly walked toward me, giving me a very confusing look, I got very scared. What had my father said or done to this man? When he finally arrived at my seat, the professor did not scold me or lecture me. Instead, he slowly reached out his hand to shake mine. He asked me how my father was and I said, "Fine, thank you." Then he asked me to tell my father that Dr. Haru says hello and he misses him.

Similar incidents happened to me several times throughout the semester, and every day grew in me the realization that I had big shoes to fill. Almost every hallway I walked and almost every leader I met would stop me to tell me stories about my father. Every story was new; my father had never told any of us how well-respected and highly admired he was. I realized I had to be the best I could be to honor God and my father. It was not easy. My first week at school I got very ill, battling to adjust to the water, food, and weather, not to mention the struggles with the language, culture shock, and the daily battles with thoughts about my family's safety.

Before I left, my father provided me with enough money for only the first semester of school. He told me, "Steve, I wish I had more money to pay for your schooling but you must trust that God has chosen you for a purpose and He will find a way for you." I could not say anything because, more than anyone, I knew how difficult things were financially for our ministries. So I nodded my head, kissed my father, and told him, "No problem."

Month after month went by, and class after class I never worried about how things would work out, I just knew that they would. I began to take things in and learn, always trying to translate what I heard into my Middle Eastern mentality. I soaked up information as fast as I could from every professor I had.

One day I got the first college bill asking me to register and pay for the second semester. I did not know what to do so

I began to pray. "God, I need You to work a miracle here. If this is really what You want me to do, if I am following Your heart and will, give me a sign so I can know." I'll never forget what happened the minute I raised my head, as tears streamed down my face. Birds started to fly down from the sky and land on the dry cement ground all around me. Well, that had definitely never happened before. So far, it has only happened once again in Jerusalem when I asked God the same question. So I met with the president of my college, Dr. Kennedy, to see what he could do to encourage me. "Well, Steven," he had said, "if you feel that God placed you here then continue your studies, be faithful, and He will open a door."

So I continued to study, living frugally, and giving every spare dollar bill to the school to pay for classes. Then one day I met a kind African gentleman who informed me about a piece of paper called a grant that I could apply for. He said the United States government sometimes likes to help college students from different countries by paying for their schooling. I could not believe my ears. This had to be God's grace!

I raced to the office where the gentleman told me the applications were. I had never heard of a grant or of the government just giving you money to attend college unless you were part of some sort of government or military organization, so I had a bit of a problem explaining what I needed. I told them I was Steven Khoury and I just wanted to fill out the papers for the government money. Fortunately, once the lady at the desk heard my name, she knew exactly what I meant. It seems she too had been touched by my father's ministry in Springfield and was more than happy to help the son of Naim (pronounced Na-eem), or "Name" as they called my father, to get through school.

From that day forward all I had to do was make a visit to the same office once a semester, fill out the grant papers, and greet the friendly lady who always inquired about my father and his ministry. The Lord had provided money for my schooling in an amazing way and I still thank Him to this day for giving me the blessing of a good education. God promises all of us that He will never leave us nor forsake us; He is always watching. I remember hearing someone say, "You are in trouble out of God's will, and are trouble in His will." And so I sought to be trouble for our spiritual enemies within God's will and planned to return to a land of many troubles, but I felt at peace knowing my mission was God's vision.

I remember hearing someone say, "You are in trouble out of God's will, and are trouble in His will." And so I sought to be trouble for our spiritual enemies within God's will.

I had left Bethlehem to go to the U.S. with three goals in mind: to get a solid Bible degree; to be ordained in a Bible-believing church; and to travel on deputation and raise support for my ministry, then head back home. I really thought about no other objectives than those and left no room for anyone or anything to interfere with my meeting those goals. While studying diligently at school I worked two regular jobs. I also drove out of state frequently, preaching in revival meetings and sharing my story with churches in different states. Soon the Lord began laying a very specific ministry on my heart for the people of Springfield. It amazed me how there were so many churches there, literally hundreds of them, and still many people did not believe.

So, together with two friends, I started a group called Warriors for Christ. This group would go down to the downtown square, which is not exactly in the best part of town, every Friday night and talk with people, telling them that Jesus loves them and that He gave His life to save them from their sin. We emphasized that, no matter what they have done or are doing, Jesus Christ can save them and right then and there they can be changed and restored. I thank God for those times. We started this group with only two, but soon more and more people wanted to share in our ministry until we had about twenty-six people spread out all over town.

Trust Your Heart

In the first semester of my senior year a friend whom I met through witnessing, named Matt, asked me to go with him to Florida for a weekend. We talked about surfing—something that has always intrigued me—some of the historic sites in St. Augustine we would like to visit, and then we talked about girls. Matt laughed and told me not to fall in love with any of his friends we would meet. He especially warned me of an exceptionally beautiful girl who was his high school yearbook editor. I remember confidently telling him, "The last thing I would think about right now is a girl. I went through three and a half years of college and never dated a girl. I have just one more semester before I return home."

I remember before I left my hometown that several of my mom's friends and relatives warned me, "Steven, do not marry a foreign girl. It is a hard culture we live in, a tough country, and worst of all they will leave you and ruin your reputation and future." Boy, did I heed those words. The last thing I wanted was for a blue-eyed monster to ruin God's ministries for me at home or my future. Those words rang in my ears through my many semesters as a college student in the U.S.

The poor girls at school probably thought I was some kind of a foreign snob but that wasn't the case. Once I got there and actually met American girls I realized that they were normal, just like everyone else. But the superstitions of the women back home had done permanent damage; I wanted nothing to do with American girls.

So off Matt and I went down to Florida. Like usual I tried my best to either drive or sleep because when I sit in the passenger's side of the car with nothing to concentrate on I tend to get carsick. Halfway down to Florida I woke up and casually looked out my window to see if the scenery had changed. Through my window I saw a beautiful, young girl driving a white Honda Civic with a surfboard hanging out of her window and a flower sticker on her windshield. And yes, I stared. I could not take my eyes off of this girl. Something attracted me to her.

On our way I asked Matt if he wouldn't mind pulling over so we could grab some drinks and get ready to hit the beach. Matt agreed, "Yeah, that is a good idea, Steve. Plus we just ran into my friend—the one I was telling you about. She'll follow us to the gas station and we can all go together."

At the time I had no idea who he was talking about. At the gas station just a mile up the road I sauntered out of the car to grab a drink—hair a mess, clothes wrinkled from sleeping in them half of the day—and saw her. It was the girl from the Civic, talking to my friend Matt! She had the same characteristics all the women back home had warned me about: light hair and light skin, blue eyes, tall and attractive. The worst kind!

I did not know what to think or say. As I walked back to the car, Matt called my name from halfway across the gas station and motioned excitedly for me to come meet his friend. What could I do? "Steve," Matt began, "this is my friend Shari, the yearbook editor I was telling you about." I tried to speak but found that my thick accent and stuttering had decided to take control of my motor skills and decrease them to nothing. In the end I finally wound up just smiling, saying hello, and darting back to the safety of my car. It was one of the most embarrassing and nervous moments of my life.

But that trip to Florida ended up being one of the best trips of my life. I had a great time, though I did wind up getting a ticket while trying to impress Shari doing "donuts" on the beach. In my defense, I did not know you could not do donuts on an abandoned beach after dark. In my hometown, you can do donuts in your living room if your car fits.

We surfed, toured, and laughed a lot on that trip. On the way to Matt's house I asked to ride with Shari. We talked for three whole hours. I had never talked so much on one trip before. Shari and I asked questions about each other's backgrounds, families, and future aspirations. That night she had to drive another hour to her hometown so we continued our conversation on the phone. We began regularly communicating by email and occasional phone calls. I jumped at every opportunity to work overtime so that I could buy more minutes to be able to get to know her better. That summer I asked Shari to come and help out in our summer camp program in Jerusalem, so she and a few other volunteers came to Israel to help us out. That was the first time I had seen her since our trip to St. Augustine.

She had the same characteristics all the women back home had warned me about: light hair and light skin, blue eyes, tall and attractive. The worst kind!

At the time I was just interested in getting to know Shari. She had quickly become a good friend. We did not even hold hands for the first year and a half that we knew each other. My conservative Middle Eastern upbringing made simple gestures like that very inappropriate for a man who hasn't even officially asked her parents their permission to date their daughter. For about two years Shari and I built a relationship over the phone. She came back to Bethlehem twice more to study Arabic and learn my culture.

After two strong, solid years we finally had that talk. Although things seemed very good for both of us, I kept fighting it, haunted by the things I had been told and taught. Even after we talked about engagement and a future together, I had many doubts. At the end of her third trip when the time came for her to leave, Shari flew back to her hometown while I stayed in Bethlehem.

Now, Middle Eastern people are known to be fantastically stubborn and I am no exception. For the next six months after Shari left I fought all sorts of fears and doubts about marriage. My mind whirled with questions: What if she left me? Could she be strong on such a hard mission field? Would she work to be an asset to our ministries here in the Middle East? My traditions and culture continued to blind me. When I talked to my parents about my predicament they told me to follow my heart. They told me I'd have troubles no matter what and that yes, marrying a foreigner would probably make those problems worse. I'd be viewed differently in the community and I'd have to teach Shari many things about our culture and traditions she did not yet know, besides the obvious language barrier. Still, they encouraged me to pray and talk to Shari to see where God would lead us.

The very next week I received a call from my younger brother, Peter, who was living and studying in Springfield, Missouri, with my middle brother, Paul. He told me that Paul had gone to California to visit our cousin, and he had become very ill and needed me there right away. So I flew out to California almost immediately to care for Paul. As soon as I arrived at my relatives' home in California and made sure my brother was okay, I began thinking about Shari. I had never thought of marrying anyone else before her. She was so kind and compassionate, such a good friend, and was even willing to live in a foreign country forever to be with me and help a people who were not her own.

Every day my brother slowly recovered, though I doubt it was because of my wonderful healing hands. Many of my nights were spent by the ocean. I would sit and stare at the gentle waves, asking God to answer the questions I had in my heart. I asked God to give me some sort of sign to show me the way.

One night I woke up at about three in the morning and began dialing Shari's home phone number. I do not know what came over me. In my culture, such an act of rudeness would be the equivalent of wearing a big sign around my neck that said, "I am a disrespectful bum. Please do not let me marry your daughter." Shari's parents answered the phone. I was so confused and nervous I began stumbling all over my words, but eventually got out that I was terribly sorry to call so early in the morning but that I had to talk to Shari urgently. Thank God her mom was nice enough not to hang up on me and agreed to put Shari on the phone.

I told Shari that Paul had a serious pneumonia and was very ill, and asked her to come to my relative's home in California so we could be together. Her wonderful parents agreed to let her come and see me. Somehow they knew that we were meant to be together, though I am not sure I saw it at the time. We had only two days before I was booked to fly back to Jerusalem. I was searching for God's sign to take away all doubt about whether Shari was my partner for life. God, however, chose this time to be silent. I could not make such a decision without His absolute assurance.

Poor Shari. She was so upset with me for those two days. After having flown across the country to be with me and talk out what we were going to do, Shari found herself back at LAX airport with no new information about our engagement status. She didn't speak to me at all during the ride to the airport, and I couldn't blame her.

After dropping her off and saying our good-byes, I drove away from the sidewalk and saw three signs up over the street bridge: Parking, Return to Terminal Gates, and Exit. As I turned to get into the Exit lane God finally spoke to my heart with a clarity that left no question in my mind. He said, "Steven, do not let her go. She is the one I have chosen for you." I believe that until that point it was my stubbornness, not God's silence, that kept me from seeing the truth before or hearing God's voice. I once heard one of my friends say, "Don't look for someone you can live with, but someone you can't live without." Without a second thought I swerved into the parking entrance, ignoring the squealing brakes and honking horns of the angry drivers behind me. I had to get to Shari! I had to find her and tell her I was sorry for being so stubborn. I had to tell her that she was the only one for me.

My destiny was to be with Shari. It is God's will for her to share in God's mission and help make a difference. Of course I could not find a parking spot anywhere, but I finally found a legal spot to squeeze my little rental car into. I knew that it was not going to be easy finding her, especially in an airport as busy as LAX. I knew that if I was going to catch her I had to run fast to find her in time. I ran to the first stairway I could find and up to the first floor, but I could not find a way over to the gate area. Those of you who have experienced the parking system in LAX know how confusing it is to get around.

I was in a hurry so I didn't have a lot of time to read signs or directions. I ran up another flight of stairs and found myself in a large, open parking lot filled with cars. Looking down, I could see people coming and going and could see the entrance area where I dropped Shari off, but I could not get to it. I ran back downstairs where there were several six-foot dividers in the parking lot blocking my way to the main entrance gate. In my state of increasing panic I found myself doing what I would normally have done in the West Bank when there is no alternative. I ran up to the first divider, reached out my right hand, and hopped over the divider. As I was running up to the second one it dawned on me that airport security guards were watching me, a young Middle Eastern man desperately running toward the gates. Oh, great. I would probably be arrested by security guards before I found Shari's gate. Then I remembered my cell phone.

I darted inside through the sliding glass doors and felt the cold whoosh of air from the overworked air-conditioning units as I heard Shari's tentative hello on the other end of the line. Before she could speak I began rapid-fire questions as I continued to weave through the people and around luggage. I asked her where she was and if she had gone through security yet. "Steve," she said, "what is it now? Just let it go. There's someone better for you in the Middle East." My heart sank. "Please, Shari," I begged, "just tell me you have not gone through security yet." She said she hadn't. When I asked her which gate she was at she begrudgingly told me. I quickly followed the signs until I spotted her. I asked God to give me the strength to tell her my heart and not to be afraid. I told Shari to turn around, that I was right behind her. I stood for a moment, bent over with my hands on my knees as I tried to catch my breath. I'm sure security was relieved but at the moment I wasn't paying attention to anyone but Shari. I told her I couldn't lose her, that she was the one and that I wanted her and only her right next to me every day for the rest of my life. Yes, I want to always be with this foreign, light-skinned, beautiful, blue-eyed girl.

We wound up having two weddings: one in Florida for her family, and another in my hometown. Naturally many of my family's friends did not like that I married a foreigner, especially since there is a seven-to-one gender ratio due to the wars. People would ask me, "Why her? Why a foreigner?" I heard the same prejudices I was told before I left to go to college. This time, however, I knew my heart and I knew God's chosen woman for my life was Shari. We knew there would be difficulties and challenges for our new lives together, but I had the blessings of my father and of Shari's parents as well, and we knew God's hand was on us. I've learned that those who do not see the big picture often get caught up with insignificant details outside of God's plans.

Trust in Your Calling

Once you give someone a chance and show them your love you'll see a different outcome. Shari is one of my heroes. She gave up her life of luxury, comfort, and freedoms to come with me to my war-torn country, to make a difference and bring the Word to the lost and dying. She didn't give up on this stubborn Palestinian, and I thank her for that. Do not ever give up on following your beliefs and the passions God lays on your heart. You will be confronted with things you could never imagine would be problem areas in your life. The question is, what are the motives behind your actions, and who are they for?

I am no expert on love; five years ago it hit me like a semi truck. I was so focused on my dreams that I had no room for anyone else in my life. I remember thinking that even the smallest distraction could compromise my mission. I've learned that without Christ, any relationship will fail. You must be open to whatever He has for you in life, and you have to be willing to listen to Him. Inner peace comes through listening to God. Accepting this and learning from it will lead to a greater understanding of how to communicate better with Him.

I believe everything happens for a reason. God has every major step in your life planned out. In everything you do, give glory to the God who created you. The one you love and admire can make you or break you and Satan knows our weak areas. He feeds off of them, strategizing and manipulating them to get us to turn from God or stop listening to Him. He confronts us with the things we cherish most and with the ones we hold dearest. I like to always spend time with the people I love. Time is running out for us and the clock is ticking here in the Middle East. Please try to love like Christ loved. When you look at the people you love, look past their flaws, especially if you expect the same for yourself. Look at the good in the ones you love. Look at them as Christ would see them. Everyone needs love.

I've learned that those who do not see the big picture often get caught up with insignificant details outside of God's plans.

I've learned something very important growing up in Bethlehem with warring groups fighting over every scrap of land they can. If you were to put me in a room filled with different kinds of people from corner to corner, we would all share a common factor. Deep down in our inner hearts and minds, we all want to be loved. No matter how big or small, tough or fragile, religious or secular, famous or infamous, we all need to be loved. *"Every day without love is a day wasted."*

"Most assuredly, I say to you, he who believes in Me, the works that I do he will do also; and greater works than these he will do, because I go to My Father. And whatever you ask in My name, that I will do, that the Father may be glorified in the Son. If you ask anything in My name, I will do it."

JOHN 14:12-14

There is a limit at which forbearance [patience] ceases to be a virtue.

JOHN BUNYAN, *PILGRIM'S PROGRESS*

CHAPTER 4

Tick-Tock

Living the Life of an Empowered Christian

FOR THE LONGEST time I prayed to God to show me how to start my own mission work in Israel and in the Palestinian territories at the same time. This is something people have been struggling to do for years. Coming straight out of college, the first thing I knew to do was to begin writing our purpose statement, trying to assemble intelligent-sounding words and a good catchphrase. But the more I thought about it, the more I realized Christ lived as a simple man and His message is one of simple grace and love. I decided to try to emulate Christ's ways of love and light in my purpose statement. What I came up with was: "Building hope in lives that lost it, planting love in hearts that forgot it, to build a better tomorrow."

As I sat in the church in Bethlehem where I grew up, I pondered these words and how I could put them into action in the new area to which I was called, Jerusalem. To me they represent giving hope through the message of Christ and showing acts of love by meeting people's physical needs in addition to helping them see their spiritual need. In this beginning process I learned that tomorrow's outcome depends on today's decisions, meaning the way you go about starting something will greatly affect its outcome.

I know the outcome of a bus bombing or a school shooting or even a home being torn down. Israel is such a small country that any problem or issue always causes a ripple effect. Many people from both sides, Israelis and Palestinians, suffer from the evil decisions of their own radicals.

Most Americans will be able to recall what they were doing at the time of terrorist attacks on the World Trade Center on 9/11, several years ago. Can you remember the effects that it had on the nation? Israel has experienced many such bombings, and the Israeli and Palestinian peoples have shared over and over those same feelings of hurt, confusion, loss, pain, and helplessness. I've always associated with the saying, "I have been building in troubled times, remodeling the minds and hearts." This saying draws me because I came to the realization that we grow and learn a lot from our mistakes, and change for the better in time.

Making Every Day Count

My sole purpose in this country is to affect as many as I can with the message of Christ. There is so much that needs to be done and with such a small Christian population there are relatively few people willing to do it. I thank God that He chose me to be one of the few willing to be used. To many people in the region I am Pastor Steve, an evangelical pastor following in his father's footsteps—sharing the message of Christ boldly just like my father taught me, and standing strong in the face of persecution when it comes.

Many people perceive my life and vision as a way to attempt to earn favor with God. They do not understand that because I am saved I already know I am going to heaven. They do not understand that I do what I do because I enjoy serving my Lord and would like to see all of them in heaven with me when I die. They do not understand the love of Christ. It is difficult to look into the eyes of those who just lost a close family member or friend to a bullet, bomb, or a stabbing, regardless of their nationality, and tell them to forgive and keep on moving forward.

Every day as I walk the streets of Bethlehem and Jerusalem, I am reminded that there are hurting people all around me. Due to years of political and religious betrayal, people of all ages are struggling to find meaning in a land of confusion. Many are walking a path of uncertainty, hoping that the next day will be a better one, yet the only answer is the true path that leads to righteousness and eternal hope in the Savior.

Everything is moving fast, built on nothing more than false hope offered by selfish motives—the result of Satan working through the minds and lives of corrupt government officials.

As the end times draw near, so does the coming of the Kingdom of God. This is why I feel such an urgency to help the people of this region to know the truth of the Messiah's death and resurrection.

The Bible says that he is the "prince of the power of the air" and "the ruler of this world." I believe that Jerusalem is God's beating heart, but I also believe it is Satan's White House. Just as the White House is the central icon for the U.S., Jerusalem is the center of importance for the fallen angels of the world. Satan knows that "where your treasure is, there your heart will be also" (Luke 12:34). And because God's heart is in Jerusalem, Satan has become its number one treasure hunter, causing trouble in every corner of the city, in every home hardening hearts and blinding eyes from seeing the truth. As the end times draw near, so does the coming of the Kingdom of God.

This is why I feel such an urgency to help the people of this region to know the truth of the Messiah's death and resurrection. I have seen lives changed so I believe in change. I have witnessed how even tragic deaths can serve to spark a passion in others, therefore I anticipate it.

I have heard that some cities in America are filled with people living in the fast lane, who never take a break or stop to think about the way they live their lives. In my country we live in the death lane, where every day could be your last. There is no guarantee that you will come home at the end of the day, nor is there a guarantee that you will find work that puts food on the table for that day. Sometimes I think the only reason people stay at all must be that they are helplessly drawn here. My family is drawn to this land to reach the lost at any cost. The rocks must not yet cry out. There are still a relatively few proclaiming the message of the risen Messiah. Those of you who have visited Israel and the West Bank have seen the cosmetically covered truth—a hurting, hungry, and lost nation waiting for the end in their own thoughts and ways. The eyes of this nation are covered by a blindfold that keeps it from seeing the truth. Isaiah 6:10 says,

> "Make the heart of this people dull, and their ears heavy, and shut their eyes; lest they see with their eyes, and hear with their ears, and understand with their heart, and return and be healed."

In conferences I am often asked, "What keeps you going? Why are you still there?" Honestly, I ask this of myself also, but every time I am able to come up with so many reasons to stay that it always seems to renew my ambitions for Christ.

Carrying a Simple Message

When I share my Savior, the reaction I get, especially from people in the Middle East, makes me jump with joy. It is sometimes difficult to share the message of Jesus Christ because of many preconceived ideas about Christianity, the sin nature of man, or hostilities toward the gospel. Yet the message is a soul-changing one and well worth the effort. Many of my people have not heard a clear, simple message of the gospel and have yet to witness firsthand what Jesus can do when they follow Him, so we need to focus on the reason for the cross. Paul said, "We preach Christ crucified... For I determined not to know anything among you except Jesus Christ and Him crucified" (1 Corinthians 1:23; 2:2).

There are several challenges that come with preaching the Word of God. I am regularly asked by youth in our ministries, "Why are we the forgotten people?" This is a question that we in leadership are hearing more and more from our Palestinian youth, both believers and nonbelievers. They ask me, "Why don't we see people reach out to our needs? Almost every day we see a helping hand being stretched out to people all around us, but we as Palestinians have no recourse." Many Palestinian Christians feel that they are alone in their struggles because of our minority status. The plea I often hear is, "Doesn't anyone know that we as Palestinian Christians exist in this country? Does anyone care for our lives and future?"

The stories you hear in the newspapers sway the court of public opinion because of the war and killing between the Palestinians and Israelis. That is why whenever a non-violent, peacekeeping Christian in the Palestinian territories or any Palestinian resident reaches out, he is often stereotyped as a freedom fighter, militant, or radical.

"Why doesn't anyone stand with us and tell us they are praying for us?" they ask. When a young girl or boy asks me this question, it feels like a dagger stabbing me in the heart every time. I know exactly what they feel and the confusion that goes through their minds. The feelings of being left behind, that everything around them is moving forward while they remain. They feel that the world is going in circles but they are standing in the same place, wondering what they can do to change their life's course and destiny.

My struggles as a Christian leader revolve around people and their needs. There isn't a day that goes by where we don't have ten, twenty, sometimes more Christians and non-Christians seeking help because they are struggling to find answers for their future, a way to put food on the table, or a way out of their physical or spiritual troubles. I often wonder whether the people I love, know, or spoke to on the street will be alive the next day. The uncertainty here is immense. There are no guarantees for either side, the Palestinians or the Israelis, which is all the more reason to stand firm and to preach the gospel of Christ. He is our only guarantee.

I have heard it said that money makes the world go 'round. From what we see of Christ's short life and ministry on earth, love and compassion toward people far outlast the longevity of money. What I have seen and experienced in the region is that the message of love and forgiveness goes a long way, far longer than the "eye for an eye and tooth for a tooth" motto that many here subscribe to. Christ's teachings on love and forgiveness are what my family and I strive to communicate to others. We remind ourselves every day that no matter what happens to us or around us we must show love and compassion. *Love makes the world go 'round.*

Understanding the Enemy

A sense of confusion and despair is in the air, with people waiting for a whisper of an elusive peace that will give all the answers. Political diplomacy driven by false motives is what's causing the ruckus in our lands. Jerusalem is Satan's playground and the people are consumed by confusing, false political prom-

Persecution in Palestinian Neighborhoods

PALESTINE MAY NOT be a country, but it is a nation of proud Muslim Arabs. Ancient in origins but created in modern-times—born in 1947 with Israel as a two-state solution to end the Arab-Israeli conflict—Palestine has seen a reversal of affluence. The nation went from occupying most of the area that is deemed the "Holy Land," to now occupying just four areas of the disputed land which includes the West Bank. The row over land ownership has left Muslims who convert to Christianity in a precarious position. Palestinian Firas tells how his family was terrorized because they are the only Christians living in a sea of Muslims.

"A pastor would come and visit us in our home and I would laugh," says Firas of his pre-conversion days. "He would say nonsense about loving your enemy and not to hate and not to kill. I thought this was ridiculous. In Palestine there is nothing but hatred and killing. I didn't take Christianity seriously. My wife asked me to come to church but I wouldn't. But she kept reading her Bible every night when she came to bed and finally, I decided to go, thinking that I would get some food afterward. Six months later I declared Jesus as my personal Savior. I believed He was my God and I decided to surrender my life to Him. Pastor Steve changed my life.

"Now we have problems with Muslim people," Firas said. "The Palestinians want the Israelis gone so they fight the *Intifada*. But we, being Christians, don't want the *Intifada*. We don't want violence, we want love. Jesus asked us to love everyone."

(continued)

(continued)

But it is difficult for a Christian in the Palestinian territories. "Whenever I send my son to the grocery store, the Muslims beat him up," says Firas. "They know he is the only Christian in the area, so they taunt him, threaten him, and hit him. We can't go anywhere or leave because Muslims are everywhere. Where would we go? We are in the fire and it is very dangerous, but Jesus is with us. This is the mission field. The work is where we need to tell about Jesus. Jesus is with us."

ises, offering them wealth, power, and modernism. We know that there will be no true peace until the Prince of Peace Himself returns; there will always be wars, fighting, and turmoil.

What determines the outcome in today's battle is whether the message of Christ is being brought before the people or not. Jesus is the only one who can make a permanent change in our nation by changing men's hearts. I have seen nothing to convince me that any other person could ever help like Christ can. We must place that option before them, whether or not they accept it. All the people talk about is peace. They must discover that Jesus Christ's work and message is the only way to true peace—not just peace in the Holy Land but, more importantly, peace with God.

The only answer to our problem is for the people to believe the message of Christ and obey the gospel. Our job is to make that message known. Satan keeps people living in anger, pride, and greed. What's worse is that Satan has every people group in this land trying to solve their problems in totally different ways. Chaos is bound to ensue in a land that does not know unity through Christ. We often look at the methods of the religious radical terrorist groups and wonder, "What on earth are they thinking? What could they possibly believe they are accomplishing?"

I believe that Satan's goal in Jerusalem is to make every church a museum, every Christian a tourist, and every soul his own Holy Land souvenir. Conflict is on the rise. Everywhere I turn I am faced with a conversation or an incident that seems to provide grounds for more and more conflict. I am always picked out of the crowd as a Christian for wearing a cross on my neck, having a Christian name, or simply being a Palestinian who walks and talks with Jewish people.

Christians around the world need a reality check, something to wake them up to the supernatural realm and help them see that Satan's power is growing stronger and his works are penetrating minds and conquering souls. It is a wonderful feeling to know that Christ has already won the war, but we must prepare the people for that victory so they don't find themselves on the losing side when the time comes. Christ's victory began here, on a cross outside the city, and it will end here, with His return. We do have an edge on Satan's plans. If we discover his strategies, we can learn to biblically counter them. The Bible teaches us, "Therefore submit to God. Resist the devil and he will flee from you" (James 4:7).

Backing down or being afraid of speaking out about Christ is like treating the defeated challenger as the champion.

To defeat an enemy you must fight him on his own turf. We here in the church are learning to acknowledge his imminent defeat and treat him like the loser he really is. Backing down or being afraid of speaking out about Christ is like treating the defeated challenger as the champion. Everyone around you has a message, a philosophy, or an input, and so should you.

Time is running out for the lost, but it is just beginning for us. We carry something that the world does not: hope in a risen Savior. The first step to resist Satan is to refuse to be a "diplomatic Christian." By accepting the fact that our faith is in direct conflict with the world's messages offered by Satan, and recognizing and accepting that being a "diplomatic Christian" is a threat to our power to share the gospel, we can begin to resist it.

Being Committed to Unity

Because we live in a radical world, we must face the world by being radical Christians. Now, I'm not talking about taking up broadswords and banners to combat the enemy, but making the truth known at every opportunity we can. According to www.religioustolerance.org, Christianity is losing almost an entire percent of its American members every year. This means that in thirty-four years non-Christians will outnumber Christians in the United States. In fact, the fastest growing religion in America is Wicca, a pagan religion that doubles its American members about every thirty months.

The fastest growing religion in the Middle East (and the world) is Islam, with about 23% of the world population following Islam. In Israel and the West Bank territories there is an estimate of less than 1.8% Christians, which the government lumps together with Jehovah's Witnesses, Maronites, and so on. Out of this percentage, only approximately 0.20% are true born-again believers.

So whose fault is this? Well, it's been a joint effort. While Christians have decided to pretend the world will find Christ on its own, Satan contents himself with letting us, as he makes his own plans. Christians sit around gossiping about the new member's sins while Satan gains ground in our government, homes, schools, and lives.

I'll never forget some of the first churches I visited while studying in the U.S. I did not know much about freedom of worship, nor did I know how outspoken one can be about his faith. I thought church in the States would be the same for me as it always was. I'd either be coming home beaten and bruised, get my Bible ripped from my hands, or be forced to worship in secret for fear of nosy neighbors. What I found was a whole different set of problems. I remember going to one church where they were remodeling and were squabbling about the color of the curtains and carpeting. At another church I found Christians arguing over who could park where in the church parking lot.

Some of the worst experiences I've ever had were in churches where members verbally attacked each other over issues like the Holy Spirit, who had the better choir, which praise instruments should be allowed, or whether PowerPoint materials were of the devil. I've also heard Christians argue over the specific wording one should use for telling someone about Jesus and which version of the Bible should be allowed in churches. I've actually heard a Christian say that any version different from his version of the Bible was Satanic.

I remember being told about a Muslim who just trusted Jesus Christ as his personal Savior. He came to Christ through a video he found lying outside a dumpster on the street. He took it home and watched it. He had never known that God Himself had died to give him assurance of eternity. After watching the tape he returned to the same dumpster to see if there were any more materials that talked about the truth of Christ. He found clumps of wet paper with typing lying around the ground. He gathered them up and took them home to dry. What he found were bits and pieces of Scripture from the four

Gospels gathered from different ripped up, burned Bibles. That man learned about Christ just as surely as reading from a nice, fancy, hand-sown leather Bible.

Becoming Radically Faithful

Even though we do not have the luxuries of life that other countries possess, as Arab Christians we are still rich at heart. There comes a sense of joy in persecution and confrontation. Remember Matthew 5:11 where Jesus says:

> "Blessed are you when they revile and persecute you, and say all kinds of evil against you falsely for My sake."

We must be radically faithful to the end, holding on with every last breath to carry this life-altering torch of victory. But you will not see me in the streets waving a ten-foot-tall Christian banner, nor will you find me wearing a placard on the side of the street screaming that sinners are going to hell. Being radically faithful is a lifestyle you adopt, not a single action. This lifestyle allows you to speak the truth about the message of Christ throughout your life no matter where you are, who you are with, or what position of power you have.

We must be willing to be martyrs. Luckily, many countries have stopped killing off their Christians, though some still do and we all suffer the losses of brothers and sisters who've chosen to die rather than conform to the religion of their neighbors. For the rest of us, telling the truth of Christ constantly will make us proper servants of God. No one wants to be on the losing end, so why not help people to be victors? Tell them about spiritual realities, and how to walk the narrow road that leads to the Champion of the winning side. That is what the famous story of *Pilgrim's Progress* was about. I loved the reality of that story.

Become radically faithful with the message of Jesus Christ. You will not back down when faced by a friend or a relative, you will not be shy about speaking out against something that hurts others' eternal destiny, you will not be afraid to speak your mind about the truth of the life of Christ, and lastly you will refuse to allow anyone to steal the joy you are entitled to.

I promised myself eight years ago, at age twenty-two, that I would enjoy the ministry God has allowed me to serve in. I will let nothing steal the joy I am entitled to, and Satan will not take what is rightfully mine. That is why I was willing to return home to Israel to help take back what is rightfully God's—the lost souls. Right before I left college I was bombarded with options; some were the opportunity of a lifetime for a young man. I do not think, however, that these doors opened to me because I was the smartest or most talented one for the job—in fact, my grades will show any doubter otherwise. I believe these doors opened to me because we have a sleepless enemy who can smell someone who is willing to compromise. I knew the consequences that faced me when I left the U.S., but I also knew what the Lord had called me to do with my life. When God sees a willing servant, He finds a willing way.

Every day I thank God for showing me He is real and working in our lives. There is no doubt in my mind that time is running out and the clock is ticking. We must seize this moment for the sake of Christ. Wherever you are on this globe, I hope and pray that you carry on with God's message. Carry the gospel news of victory with confidence that we are on the winning side. Stay strong and do not ever give up, because Jesus loves you. Just look at His hands and feet; you mean the world to Him, and He should mean the world to you.

Jesus, our Master, was a realist. Jesus never called those who followed Him to live in denial or to live with their heads in the sand.

CHARLES STANLEY

Do not be conformed to this world, but be transformed by the renewing of your mind.

ROMANS 12:2

CHAPTER 5

Confrontational Conversations

*Diplomatic Answers Can
Be a Stumbling Block*

SOMEONE ONCE told me, "Let's take God out of the box. Let's not limit Him. Can't we be just a little bit more open-minded?" He was referring to what he thought was the narrow-minded Christian view that there is only one way to God. He thought it was a hypocritical stance for Christians to take, since we preach that God is all-merciful. I curtly replied, "How 'bout we try leaving God in the position of authority He commands and not try telling an all-knowing, perfectly righteous Being how He should grant the mercy we don't deserve?"

There Is Only One Path to God

Why do we expect God to bend His perfection for our convenience? Why is it so hard for us to see Him as the ultimate Redeemer of the darkest speck of dust in the galaxy? Do not try to change God to conform to your opinions of what God should or should not do. Do not try to drag God down to your limited perspective of life. We must be willing to accept God where He is and how He is. In Israel and the Palestinian territories, Christians are always expected to get out of their box and accept everyone else's opinions as valid and equal to God's Word.

I once met a Jewish rabbi who wished to discuss the differences between Christianity and Judaism with me. He wanted to be diplomatic by concentrating on how much the Jews and Christians are alike. He said the only real difference is our opinion on Jesus as the Messiah and the following of the Hebrew commandments. This rabbi actually said that all paths lead to God. All we must do is follow His commandments, he said, adding that Christians, Jews, and Muslims are all good people—we just need to live peacefully and accept each other. Even though I agree with a lot of what the rabbi was saying, I couldn't resist. I asked him, "Well, what if that is not true? What if there is one message, and that message is that repenting of sin and trusting in Jesus Christ is the only way to truth and God's salvation?" The rabbi told me that it was a little too judgmental to think that the answer to everything is Jesus Christ. He told me that views like mine were why there was so much violence in our country. Then he repeated the same sentiments about not limiting the Almighty to a box.

I asked him, "Well, whose box are you referring to? Yours, mine, or the Muslims'?" I asked him the same question: "Why don't we try accepting God's choices on how to show His mercy and judgment?" Of course, he did not have an answer to that because, as a Jew, he knew he could not presume to tell God what He can or cannot do. The Old and New Testaments' truths about the way of redemption, which is Jesus Christ the prophesied Messiah, are clearly marked from the beginning of the Torah to the end of the Book of Revelation.

Sharing the Truth Is a Matter of Life and Death

Many wonderful people I met have shied away from me when they realize that they can't discuss Christ with me and expect me to be politically correct. When asked a question like, "Hey, Steve, aren't our prophet and God the same as yours?" or "Hey, Steve, who do you pray to? Don't the saints hear our prayers and report to the Father our specific needs?" or, "Doesn't God hear and accept everyone as long as they believe in a god?" I will not betray my Savior to give them a diplomatic answer. I tell them the truth as the Bible tells it and try to show them as much Scripture as I can to back my beliefs.

These are the kinds of questions often asked of Christians, yet when we answer with biblical truth we are chastised for it. I have two close Muslim friends. One of them once came to me to talk about our friend Mo, whom I had recently spoken to about the gospel. He immediately began firing questions at me about why I felt I had to offend Mo with my religious views. "I thought he was one of your good friends," he scolded me, "and now you've gone and insulted him too." The problem with this accusation, however, was that it was Mo himself who began our conversation about Christ. He asked, and I told him who Jesus really is and shared the gospel with him. Mo knew my strong Christian convictions. If he didn't want to hear about it, I am confident that he wouldn't have asked. Mo wanted answers to questions deep down. He wanted to know how a person he knew so well could believe that the only way to God and heaven was through Jesus Christ.

This mediating friend then countered, "Well, Steve, you could have done a couple of things differently." I was intrigued. I asked my friend what I could have possibly done to make it easier. He told me I should have changed the subject, ignored the question, or simply told him that God accepts us all as human beings and that's good enough. I told him that no friendship was worth the betrayal of my Savior. In fact, I had shared Christ's message so thoroughly because he was a good friend and I hoped and prayed that I would someday see him in heaven. I told him Jesus Christ offers the only salvation, that we must turn from our sin and trust in Christ, believing that He and the Father are one. I told him that this was the only way to lead a blessed life and spend eternity in heaven. I could not get a word out of him. I wish I could have, but all he could do was stare into my eyes, disgusted with my stubborn passion for Christ.

Later that day I called Mo and apologized if he thought I was belligerent or rude. I also told Mo that Jesus Christ loved him so much that He came down to earth to pay for his sin by dying on the cross. I told him Jesus has the only answer to everyone's sin problem, and will give forgiveness to those who trust Him. Before I hung up I reminded my friend how much I loved him as a good friend and human being and that I would never wish him harm, that I only wanted to share with him the water that quenches all thirst.

"When you came out straight to my face and told me passionately about your Savior, I was shocked because I had never heard an answer like that before."

After that conversation Mo did not get in contact with me for months. Then a few months later my phone rang. It was Mo. "Hey, Steve," he said, "I have to see you right now—it's life and death." I could tell from his voice that something was seriously wrong. Still, I wondered why he would call me in a life-and-death situation. Was it just a trap?

I drove immediately to the town where he lived. As I pulled up I asked Christ to give me strength. Walking toward the house, I noticed that the front doors were open but the windows were shut. The front room was dark and silent. As I slowly walked in step by step, looking around all the corners in the room and wondering if anyone was there in the darkness, I heard Mo's voice in the corner. I stopped immediately and looked over to where Mo's voice was coming from. "Steve, I am so glad you came. I have been going through many problems in my life with no hope, no joy, and no peace. Every day I wake up wondering why I am alive and what future there is for me. Where do I go next?

"Nothing has worked out in my life. Steve, I've become an alcoholic. Today I chose to kill myself. I put my knife to my neck and screamed out for God to forgive me because I have become nothing and I have failed Him. I cried, 'God, if You are real, show me who You are.'" Mo paused, then continued, "The moment I asked God to show me, I felt a hand grab my right hand away from my neck, stopping my knife from harming me. The words *love* and *forgiveness* flooded my mind, and your name came to me all at once. The hand dropped the knife and laid it down on the table in front of me. Here it is, Steve—the knife."

I could see some of Mo's neck hair on the edge of the knife and the red line of blood on his neck. I told him I believed him. Mo told me that when he confronted me a few months earlier about who the true God was, I was only one of many people he had been questioning. He wanted to hear a convincing answer, but no one else would tell him anything because everyone was scared to be different or wrong.

He said, "When you came out straight to my face and told me passionately about your Savior, I was shocked because I had never heard an answer like that before. I was mad but at the same time happy that at least someone came out and told me what he thinks could change my life. After I went home I thought a lot about what you said, that it is as simple as trusting Jesus and believing in Him. But when you called to tell me that you loved me and that Jesus loves me also, I saw and heard something that I never heard or saw before—that was truth in love. Thanks to your love and faith in your Savior, you saved my life today. Please tell me, what can I do to receive joy? How can I have the forgiveness that you talked about?"

I told him that the first step we'd take would be to move his knife away from him and especially me. When I went to put the knife away in the kitchen I was shocked to find Mo's aunt scared and crying, huddled in the corner alone. I told her it was okay and that she could join us at the table if she wanted to become a new person in Christ and experience forgiveness and joy too. That moment we all got on our knees right there in the living room. I told Mo that Jesus was the one who stopped him from killing himself that day. All he had to do now was call out to Him and receive Him into his life and let Him be number one. That day both repented of their sins and asked Jesus Christ to be the Lord of their lives. Today Mo lives in Europe and is working, enjoying God, and loving the Lord every day of his life. Glory to Jesus. He is there knocking; all we have to do is let Him in.

I thank God that I didn't miss out by not standing up for my faith or being a diplomatic Christian. Think of the blessings I would have robbed Mo from experiencing by not telling him about the change that Christ caused in my life—it would have literally meant his death, here and in eternity. When you are a diplomatic Christian, you are diplomatically robbing a hungry soul of eternal life.

You cannot keep what is not yours to contain, so give the message out every chance you get, especially when you are confronted with it. You might never know what that person's reason is for asking the question, or what he is going through or facing. I mentioned in earlier chapters that I passed many sleepless nights when the only thought on my mind was whether I would make it through that night.

My Heroes Are Three Jewish Men

One of the few ways I was able to calm my mind and spirit during times of war or intentional attacks was to talk to God and read His promises. I love that my Savior is faithful and honest, true to His promise to never leave us or forsake us. When confrontation knocked on the door of three Jewish men in the Old Testament, God was clearly with them—and the result of their strong, firm beliefs was to turn the eyes of the nation to the one true God. I cannot help getting excited about confrontation and persecution. The story of Shadrach, Meshach, and Abed-Nego serves as an example for us, so we'll be examining it in the next few chapters.

When you are a diplomatic Christian, you are diplomatically robbing a hungry soul of eternal life.

Read this story in Scripture with me where we see confrontation and persecution manifested through the lives we find in Daniel 3:1–16:

> ¹Nebuchadnezzar the king made an image of gold, whose height was sixty cubits and its width six cubits. He set it up in the plain of Dura, in the province of Babylon. ²And King Nebuchadnezzar sent word to gather together the satraps, the administrators, the governors, the counselors, the treasurers, the judges, the magistrates, and all the officials of the provinces, to come to the dedication of the image which King Nebuchadnezzar had set up. ³So the satraps, the administrators, the governors, the counselors, the treasurers, the judges, the magistrates,

and all the officials of the provinces gathered together for the dedication of the image that King Nebuchadnezzar had set up; and they stood before the image that Nebuchadnezzar had set up. ⁴Then a herald cried aloud: "To you it is commanded, O peoples, nations, and languages, ⁵that at the time you hear the sound of the horn, flute, harp, lyre, and psaltery, in symphony with all kinds of music, you shall fall down and worship the gold image that King Nebuchadnezzar has set up; ⁶and whoever does not fall down and worship shall be cast immediately into the midst of a burning fiery furnace."

⁷So at that time, when all the people heard the sound of the horn, flute, harp, and lyre, in symphony with all kinds of music, all the people, nations, and languages fell down and worshiped the gold image which King Nebuchadnezzar had set up.

⁸Therefore at that time certain Chaldeans came forward and accused the Jews. ⁹They spoke and said to King Nebuchadnezzar, "O king, live forever! ¹⁰You, O king, have made a decree that everyone who hears the sound of the horn, flute, harp, lyre, and psaltery, in symphony with all kinds of music, shall fall down and worship the gold image; ¹¹and whoever does not fall down and worship shall be cast into the midst of a burning fiery furnace. ¹²There are certain Jews whom you have set over the affairs of the province of Babylon: Shadrach, Meshach, and Abed-Nego; these men, O king, have not paid due regard to you. They do not serve your gods or worship the gold image which you have set up."

¹³Then Nebuchadnezzar, in rage and fury, gave the command to bring Shadrach, Meshach, and Abed-Nego. So they brought these men before the king. ¹⁴Nebuchadnezzar spoke, saying to them, "Is it true, Shadrach, Meshach, and Abed-Nego, that you do not serve my gods or worship the gold image which I have set up? ¹⁵Now if you are ready at the time you hear the sound of the horn,

flute, harp, lyre, and psaltery, in symphony with all kinds
of music, and you fall down and worship the image
which I have made, good! But if you do not worship, you
shall be cast immediately into the midst of a burning
fiery furnace. And who is the god who will deliver you
from my hands?"

16Shadrach, Meshach, and Abed-Nego answered and
said to the king, "O Nebuchadnezzar, we have no need
to answer you in this matter."

We don't know for sure whether the image was of Nebuchadnezzar or something else, but according to the *KJV
Prophecy Study Bible:*

> The inauguration of the first Gentile Empire of Nebu-
> chadnezzar's vision was marked by the enforced public
> worship of a golden image created by King Nebuchad-
> nezzar. The golden image may have been human in form,
> though probably not a likeness of the king himself.[1]

Perhaps the king's agenda was to please his gods in fear
that their anger would befall him and his people. This story
tells us that when the trumpets and music were sounded every
human being in the empire bowed down except for three
young Jewish men who stood out like sore thumbs. Imagine
thousands of heads and knees bowing to this image, and seeing these three men staring and watching the people around
them. This was a strong testament to the truth they held so
dear in their hearts. They could have decided to go along with
everyone else and obey the commandment of the king, but
they knew this was idolatry and a betrayal of Jehovah. I could
even imagine other Jewish people or friends telling them it
was not worth getting killed over or drawing attention to

---

1 Grant Jeffrey, *KJV Prophecy Study Bible* (Grand Rapids, MI: Zondervan Pub-
lishing House, 1998), Daniel 3:1 comment, p. 958.

themselves, that God would understand their situation. This sounds a lot like what I have heard Christians say both in the Middle East and in the West.

In v. 12 we see Shadrach, Meshach, and Abed-Nego boxed in by Chaldean enemies who did not like them or their God. The Chaldeans report them to the king and manipulate him by appealing to a subject that was very sensitive to the king— his ego. These men refused to obey him. Why would these Chaldeans choose to ignore the whole nation and concentrate on these three men? Was it because the three were Jewish? Because they chose to be rebels? The Jewish men wanted to stand firm in what they believed and were not afraid to let the whole nation know that they stood for their God.

The King Wanted a Diplomatic Answer

Shadrach, Meshach, and Abed-Nego were a threat to the kingdom as well. The Chaldeans saw something in these men that scared them. They saw potential in their message. Satan knows a threat when he sees one. When the Chaldeans saw these three men they knew if these men were crazy enough to stand up among thousands, they were confident to stand up against the ultimate powers of the land. As we continue to read on through vv. 13–15, we start to see diplomatic tolerance take place. The king pulls his diplomatic card on Shadrach, Meshach, and Abed-Nego. In the beginning the king seems to think that perhaps this occurrence was a mere misunderstanding, asking them, "Is it true?" He could not comprehend that these Jews were not going to be diplomatic but were intent on being confrontational because of a conviction in their hearts.

The king seems perplexed that those whom he knew for many years, those whom he took care of and protected in his kingdom, would disobey him over such a silly matter. He believed there was no need for this entire confrontation. If the

Jewish men did indeed refuse to bow the first time, he felt it was not a large transgression, but did insist again that they bow. What the king wanted was for Shadrach, Meshach, and Abed-Nego to deny what they were confident in, something that changed their lives forever. It is interesting to see the mind of the king develop through his confusion and frustrations with some of his favorite men.

He was willing to give them another chance to obey, if they were ready, to show everyone in his palace that all is well and that the issue has been resolved. It seems the king has never seen faith and commitment like this and was caught off guard. But at the end of v. 15 something about the three Jewish men pushes the king to the limit, especially when he realizes that his diplomatic approach is not getting him anywhere, and he again threatens them with fire if they refuse to obey his new law.

> *The Jewish men wanted to stand firm in what they believed and were not afraid to let the whole nation know that they stood for their God.*

Let Nothing Hold You Back from the Truth

We have many people like King Nebuchadnezzar in Jerusalem and the West Bank territories—they are out to attack and destroy anyone whose message is different from their own, especially when that message is changing lives. Every day I am faced with the reality that this day could be the last time I will ever see my wife and my family. Every day I make sure to kiss my beautiful wife and touch base with my parents and brothers to let them know how much I love them and appreciate them. If we were to count how many times our church building in Bethlehem was bombed over the years by Molotov cocktails and hand bombs, it would total about fourteen times. I remember that while growing up, in an average Sunday service we would begin the music and four or five men might enter our sanctuary, throwing rocks at us as we worshiped the Lord.

I remember helping some of our church men to fill buckets with water to place at the front of the church near the altar. When the Molotov cocktails would start a fire we would jump to the buckets of water and put the fire out. Then we would get back to worshiping the Lord and praising Him even louder to show the men outside that we were not intimidated.

We would let nothing steal our joy, no matter what. This group once dragged my father out of the church building and took him to the street. The sounds of fists and sticks hitting my father's body still ring in my ear; I was only about eleven years old. I remember trying to climb over the church wall as I called out to my father over the ten-foot-high walls separating the church from the street. As they were beating him, they mocked him and screamed at him to stop preaching. The fact that I could not see him but could hear his body being beaten and could hear the mocking was a lot worse than the flying rock that split my head open that day, sending my father's cries into a fuzzy oblivion. Satan shows no mercy to his enemies. All who serve Christ have Satan as their enemy, and every Christian should be on the lookout for his corruption.

A while back I began to talk with a person from another faith about who Christ is and the purpose of the cross. This person had many questions on his mind and was very thirsty to learn so I was willing to share everything I could. As his speech and views began to change, his family found out and decided to teach me a lesson. A few of his friends and cousins met me at a street corner, beat me, and shoved me in a trash can. They told me to never again approach any of their families with my message. I could not speak much as I was trying to catch my breath and wriggle out of the closed trash can, but if I could have said something I would have told them there was room for them and their relatives in the family of Christ any time. There is a quote that I heard once by Emiliano Zapata, a Mexican revolutionary: "It's better to die on your feet, than to live on your knees." Well, where faith is concerned, I'd rather live on my knees in prayer than die on my feet doing nothing.

I thank God for every day that He has given me to live in this region. I am in the Lord's army. I have a message for those who want to hear, and I am not afraid to speak it. It is not a secret, I will not tweak it to make you feel better, and you'll know the effect of truth when you accept it. We all were created with a plan and that plan includes the blessings of God's presence and protection for those who trust Him. We must stand strong even when it feels that we are all alone; Christ is always with us and He promised to reward our endurance. Revelation 2:10 says:

> "Do not fear any of those things which you are about to suffer. Indeed, the devil is about to throw some of you into prison, that you may be tested, and you will have tribulation ten days. Be faithful until death, and I will give you the crown of life."

No matter where you are on this earth, Christ is right there with you. Don't ever forget that, especially when walking down paths of tribulations. *Trust in the risen Savior.*

If you read history you will find that the Christians who did most for the present world were precisely those who thought most of the next. It is since Christians have largely ceased to think of the other world that they have become so ineffective in this.

C. S. LEWIS

Therefore, if anyone is in Christ, he is a new creation; old things have passed away; behold, all things have become new.

2 CORINTHIANS 5:17

CHAPTER 6

My True Identity

Finding Your True Identity
in a Relationship with God

AS WE CONTINUE to look at the passage in Daniel 3, we see that Shadrach, Meshach, and Abed-Nego's identities were crystal clear; they were servants of the God of Israel and would worship no other gods but Him. I love the reply they give the king in v. 16: "O Nebuchadnezzar, we have no need to answer you in this matter." What they are saying here is: We know that you want us to answer you according to what you are used to, but we are not going to be diplomatic and are not worried about the consequences of our reply. We will not betray our Lord and God.

Below I would like to share with you some of the ways that our identity can become clear as believers. I want to challenge you to think these through, and realize that without knowing who you are, how will you know who you have to be as a servant of God?

1. Identify with God's Purpose in Your Life

The three men go on to say in v. 17, "If that is the case, our God whom we serve is able to deliver us from the burning

fiery furnace, and He will deliver us from your hand, O king."
I admit it: I'm very jealous of their faith and boldness. They
stared death straight in the face, turning history and a whole
empire around. The reality of confronting death and persecution did not faze them. They were confident that their God
would deliver them, even from a burning fire.

These three did not care what the enemy was planning.
They knew where they were going and they were confident in
who was meeting them on the other side of death. I wonder
what was going on in their heads. There is something else
here, though, something that people often miss when reading
this passage. They make a statement in v. 18: "But if not, let
it be known to you, O king, that
we do not serve your gods, nor will
we worship the gold image which
you have set up." Those first three
words, "But if not," offer a level of
understanding to us as we read.
You see, these men were in touch
with reality.

They knew where they were going and they were confident in who was meeting them on the other side of death.

They knew that God was all-
powerful and totally capable of
saving their lives. However, they
understood that God's plan will be carried out, and if this
meant that they would burn, then they would burn for the
glory of God.

Can you see their passion and faith? Even before they were
bound they wanted to be sure the king knew that, regardless
of what God decided to do with their lives, they would be
faithful to Him. There is great power in the words of the three
men. My father and I have been called Zionists for preaching
and teaching "love your enemies and love your neighbor as
yourself," which is not a particularly good label when you are

attempting to reach a nation divided into different pockets of religion.

We are challenged by people to show them from Scripture where it says that we must love our enemies and our neighbors as ourselves. They challenge us on the issue of the right for Israel and the Jewish people to exist in the Middle East. This question always puts us in a very difficult position as to what to say, as they are challenging our true identity. Let me explain. Being an Arab who believes in Jesus Christ and is evangelizing others is itself a difficult identity. Then to add to that, I am not well received by nominal Christians as I am considered a traitor for leaving the traditional Orthodox church. On top of that I am an Arab Palestinian living in the Arab Palestinian territories teaching that we must love the Jewish people as our neighbors and that we cannot deny the promises given to them by God more than four thousand years ago. I must state my Christian faith, and I must stand for what the Bible says.

2. Identify with Salvation

What do I say to an angry mother who just buried her young son, who was blown up by a tank simply for walking down the road at the wrong time? Or to a crying father who lost his daughter to a bus bombing while going to school? To those who believe a martyr who takes other peoples' lives is pleasing God, how do I form the right words to explain that he is a murderer and is not saving his soul? Many are tempted to jump to the "collateral damage" excuse, or say it is just God's will, or start questioning whose fault it is. Even though we must speak the truth, which is often a very hard truth especially in my country, we must speak it in love and compassion. I would like to speak more truth to you regarding salvation and the identity of those who can receive it.

It is critical to believe in the whole Bible. My father always says, "The Old Testament alone is half the truth and so is the New Testament. Now, the Old and New Testaments read together are the whole and complete truth." If you study from Scripture in Genesis 12, for example, we see God showing favor to the Jews. When everyone else was worshiping graven images or celestial bodies, the Jewish nation was worshiping the true living God. Now, granted, they did mess up and turn from God on many occasions, but they kept coming back. The Jews are not any better than the Palestinians and neither are the Palestinians any better than the Jews. When anyone, Jew or Palestinian, breaks God's commandments, he must repent and turn to Jesus. I love both and respect both as living, breathing human beings, regardless of personal circumstances.

According to God's Word, both Jew and Gentile need to trust Jesus Christ as their personal Savior. I love this passage directed at the Jews and the Gentiles in Romans 10:11–13:

> For the Scripture says, "Whoever believes on Him will not be put to shame." For there is no distinction between Jew and Greek, for the same Lord over all is rich to all who call upon Him. For "whoever calls on the name of the LORD shall be saved."

3. Identify the World's Need for Answers

When I am asked a question about rights to the land of Israel and the Jewish people, I turn to the Word of God and let Scripture speak for itself. Reading passages like Genesis 12 and 17, Isaiah 19, and many more teach me a clear message about the future of our nation and region, which again is not an easy position to hold given that I am an Arab living and ministering on the Arab side. Identifying answers to questions sometimes leads us to hear things we do not want to hear. This makes me think about Acts 5:29: "Peter and the other apostles

answered and said: 'We ought to obey God rather than men.'"
The apostles had a clear view of the message of Christ and the
commands of God. I pray we all follow that same motto by
pleasing God rather than disobeying His teachings.

The life of the three godly Jewish men in Daniel 3 clearly
shows their message: There is only one true God and we will
bow to no other. Why are issues such as faith, land, and politics
such a hot topic in the country of Israel and in the Palestinian
territories? Mankind is universally searching for answers to
why we're here and where we're going, and hoping for a guarantee of life. If we look at King Nebuchadnezzar and the people
of the Babylonian empire, they tried to appease all the gods so
they would have a better chance of a secured afterlife. The
three Jewish men were different because they were willing to
be faithful to one true God for their salvation rather than to
leave their souls to the gods' popular vote in heaven and hope
they won.

I'll never forget a confrontation I had one day with a friend
at school. He would sit at our lunch table and mock Jesus,
saying He was not the God-man crucified for the sins of the
world. He would go into what he thought was the self-evident
logic that God cannot and would not become a man just to
die at the hands of human beings. Many of the other guys at
school would hear him talking and come to see how I would
answer him. I always had the same answer; I told him Jesus
Christ loved him so much that He would die for his sins to
give him life eternal. "He changed my life," I would say, "and
He can do the same for you if you repent and believe in
Him." That reply always angered Alee, to the point that sometimes I had to face some of his friends and relatives after
school. But someone at my school had to tell him the truth.
He needed to hear the answer from someone and he seemed
to enjoy asking me.

The Bible has proven to change lives when nothing else could. It has also proven that when you search it, it will answer your questions, and when you're ready it will save you. Find your identity by finding the answer to all your questions; it lies within the Word of God.

4. Identify with People's Pain

In 2004 my wife and I began the only church in the area northeast of Jerusalem, and one of the first public outreaches we started was a woman's program for character and faith building. Out of the fifteen ladies who began to attend our meetings, I could not help noticing one specific lady. She was about twenty-seven years of age, but looking at her you would think she was in her late thirties. There was neither smile nor any joy in her life, and it was hard not to notice that this woman had it rough.

I began to explain to her that we are living in a world that is ruled by Satan, and his goal is to separate us from the grace of God. But despite our problems, the promise is that Christ brings true joy and hope when we trust in Him, and He is worth being faithful to. She mentioned to me that she and her husband were having many problems and that their family was about to split up. She had two girls and three boys all under the age of nine. I asked her what had happened, and she informed me that her husband was choosing to convert to another faith and deny Christ. I asked her why she thought he had chosen this and she replied that he believed he had found the truth.

I knew her husband and asked if I could talk to him personally. I was the second person who knew about the decision he was about to make. In our country, to change your religion is a disgrace and a betrayal to your family, friends, and honor. In some instances it also means death for the person who converts, so his decision would potentially cause many people in his family to split or fight. I went to his house for the first time and as I stood at the door knocking I asked Jesus to cover his house and my steps into it. As the man opened the door he greeted me with a hug and a traditional kiss on the cheek and welcomed me in.

We began to talk about the country and what is happening with politics, but as I looked into his eyes I couldn't help it, I just came out and asked him. I tend to wear my emotions on my sleeve, which is why I'm so bad at beating around the bush or being diplomatic, which turned out to be a great blessing as I grew older. I asked him, "What do you see in this new religion that you are seeking to dedicate your life to that you did not see in Christ? What drew you to it and convinced you to believe in it, even though you grew up in the Christian faith?" I asked him, "What would make you say no to Jesus and yes to another faith?"

In our country, to change your religion is a disgrace and a betrayal to your family, friends, and honor. In some instances it also means death for the person who converts.

The first thing he began to talk about was science and history. I could see from his replies that he had memorized some facts and spilled them out in order. Now, remember, I was not there to debate with him; I wanted to hear his heart and get to the root of things. Some of the things he mentioned were the feeling of brotherhood (something Islam is known for, where you are not alone and if you fall someone is sure to stand with you regardless); God's judgment (that He sentences to death those who disobey Him); God's Supremeness (that no one can know Him or His thoughts or plans); and God's "snotty" attitude toward humanity (that we are all unworthy). He also mentioned that man cannot save man. As I listened to his points, I could see that the love and grace of Jesus Christ had been missing in his life. Because of some pain, confusion, and trials in his life, he didn't understand who God really was or the identity he could have if he surrendered his life to Christ. Through this painful experience, his wife was able to find true grace. Her faith and walk with Christ grounded her strongly, shaping her identity in Christ.

5. Identify with the Love of Jesus

When he was through explaining himself, I thanked him for taking the time to share his heart with me and said I was there to tell him Jesus Christ is alive today. I told him, "He is here with us tonight. He turned my life around and gave me peace that passes all understanding, something that no one else can do except Him. The true Christ that I know is real and loves you the same way He loves me. The reason He died on the cross to pay for your sin is because He loved you before you ever loved yourself. Keep this in your heart."

Before I left that night, I asked him if I could pray in his home. As the words began spouting from my mouth I knew immediately that the prayer came from the Lord. "Dear God," I began, "we love You because You loved us. Thank You for making Yourself available to us in the flesh. Lord, I want to ask You to reveal Your love to my friend and his family to remind this home of Your grace. Give this home the understanding of Your cross so that they might feel Your presence in their lives. I love You and thank You for what You will do for this family, in Jesus Christ's name we ask. Amen."

I left that night not knowing what was going to happen or the result of my visit. A few days went by without hearing anything back from the family. By the end of the week I received a call from his wife saying that her husband wished to see me again. That night I went back to visit with him and he told me that his decision to convert has become known in public and the past couple of days people had been going in and out of his house trying to convince him that what he was doing was wrong and embarrassing.

He had told everyone else the same thing he'd told me. I asked him why he wished to see me again then, and he said that he was frustrated with how I reacted to his questions. He said some of the men who came to him over the past few days came with books or were refuting points. Some answered his questions and they debated for hours. "Something shocked me, though," he said. "Honestly, I am more than ever convinced to follow this new religion. But you, on the other hand, never tried to fight me or refute my questions. Instead, you listened and closed with your statement that Jesus Christ loves me and He is able to change my life." He told me that those few words had been replaying over and over in his head and that the statement I made to him shook his mind and confidence like no other. Then it dawned on me: this man had never been saved to begin with. What draws people to Christ is His love and grace through the work of the cross.

I told him, "You aren't converting from one religion to another. What you are doing is choosing your first religion, just like a baby chooses to take his first step. To start with, you never really had a true faith identity because you never knew Christ; if you did, you would know and understand grace and love, especially through the life of Christ. I cannot force you to choose but I am telling you that I and many others have chosen Christ because He is real. He died, rose again, and is coming back soon to take His followers home. It is a simple message with a simple Savior."

In the end this woman's husband followed through with his decision to choose a new faith, but I still refuse to be diplomatic. He constantly keeps in touch with me, asking me questions about the love of Christ. According to him I am the only person he allows to talk to him about the risen Christ. I believe that the battle for his family is not yet finished. I will not give up on this man. I do not consider myself any kind of genius in apologetics, especially when trying to put my words into English, but I look at the message of Christ's life as a simple one, so I speak it in a simple manner. It changed my life; I know it can change the life of anyone who chooses to trust in Christ.

6. Identify with Your Power Over Satan

This man's story is a lot like the lives of the people of Babylon, described in Daniel 3, who never thought to stop and think if there was more to "religion" than just rituals. People have to open their eyes and see the love and forgiveness of the true God. But our wise God placed three simple Jewish believers in the midst of that lost empire to show them the power of a caring, sovereign God. When people serve God, however, Satan notices. The Bible goes on to tell us that King Nebuchadnezzar's expression was changed toward the three men (v. 19), and he ordered his furnace to be heated to extreme temperatures to emphasize his fury with his disobedient subjects.

> Then Nebuchadnezzar was full of fury, and the expression on his face changed toward Shadrach, Meshach, and Abed-Nego. He spoke and commanded that they heat the furnace seven times more than it was usually heated.

It is amazing how angry our enemy gets when he does not get his way, especially when he thinks that his plan is failproof. When the men firmly refuse his command, the infuriated king demands that they be thrown into the burning fiery furnace. God allowed King Nebuchadnezzar to test the three Jewish men so that God's perfect plan could come into place. Nothing happens to God's children unless it is in His will.

These three men obeyed God, knowing that in death they would achieve life. They were courageous and bold. We must ask ourselves, "What am I doing on earth to aid my Savior in heaven?" Every day is closer to eternity, but we seem to still consume ourselves with our own needs and greed. Since we live in a world run by evil and wickedness, there is always room for light, even when it is only a little light. Drama is allowed in our daily lives, so that we might always remember to turn to Christ. Everything happens for a reason.

> We must ask ourselves, "What am I doing on earth to aid my Savior in heaven?" Every day is closer to eternity, but we seem to still consume ourselves with our own needs and greed.

This is why I am not mad or disappointed, for example, that my trip to Jordan in 2006 did not work out. My best friend, Bassem, and I were going to take a two-stop trip. Our first stop was in Jordan for a conference and our second trip was to Egypt where we were to meet some long-time friends we had not seen in years. We sent in our paperwork and waited for a reply from the visa department and decided on the hotels and details of our trip.

We were going to have a great time in two of our meetings. Usually visas take seven to ten days, so we sent our applications in three weeks earlier. We waited every day and as our time got closer we would make phone calls to make sure everything was going well and our papers were in order. It wasn't until a few days before our travel dates that we began to be concerned. It turns out that once we called the head offices to find out if there was a problem, they discovered that they did not have our papers on file.

It was as if the papers never even existed. We tried to send some faxes requesting that the issue be resolved, hoping that we could find a solution by the time we left. The day before our scheduled departure date we decided that it was not going to work out. We were disappointed, but I felt there was some special reason why things did not work out. The night before as I was unpacking my suitcase I began my pity party, trying hard not to be too disappointed. "Steven," I told myself, "do not be disappointed. God has a reason for all this. Be faithful and be thankful that an opportunity such as this even opened up at all." As I went to bed I remember saying, "Lord, I trust in You no matter what."

> *Satan wanted to get rid of us, but God has a perfect plan . . . He has the perfect number of days for our lives.*

I woke up late that morning to my phone ringing. As I reached over to answer it I realized there were about ten missed calls from a number of people. I did not think anything of it because I get a lot of phone calls. Everyone thought that we had left the country and gone to Jordan. That day the Holiday Inn in Amman, Jordan, was bombed by terrorist bombers. The whole lobby and the first and second floors of the building were completely destroyed. Our reservation was at the Holiday Inn in Amman, Jordan, first floor, near the lobby.

I, of course, had no idea what had been going on. I was alarmed when I finally scooted out of bed, turned on the lights in my dark room, stepped outside the door, and proceeded to be half-tackled by my mother, crying out thanks to God that I was here and alive. "What's the matter?" I asked her with a yawn. My mother grabbed my head in her hands and forced me to look at the TV in the living room where big red letters flashed across the bottom of the screen:

URGENT NEWS: BOMB KILLS
MANY IN AMMAN, JORDAN

That whole week the entire border of Jordan closed down.

I like to think of myself as being very blessed that God would find the time in His busy schedule, out of billions of people, to save us from getting killed. Satan wanted to get rid of us, but God has a perfect plan. We are reminded in Romans 8:35–39:

> Who shall separate us from the love of Christ? Shall tribulation, or distress, or persecution, or famine, or nakedness, or peril, or sword? . . . For I am persuaded that neither death nor life, nor angels nor principalities nor powers, nor things present nor things to come, nor height, nor depth, nor any other created thing, shall be able to separate us from the love of God which is in Christ Jesus our Lord.

God promised that He would never leave us nor forsake us. He never has and never will. We must keep our eyes on Him. He has the perfect number of days for our lives.

As we look even deeper into the passage of Daniel 3:20–23, we see a miracle manifest itself before kings and rulers. After King Nebuchadnezzar's diplomatic dialogue with the Jewish men failed, he turned to force and persecution. He thought that threats would weaken their spirit. He thought that public humiliation and a display of the strength of the fire would cause a compromise, but that also failed. He thought that by heating up the fire seven times hotter it would not only get rid of this pesky obedience problem, but also be an example to the rest of the kingdom.

> ²⁰And he commanded certain mighty men of valor who were in his army to bind Shadrach, Meshach, and Abed-Nego, and cast them into the burning fiery furnace. ²¹Then these men were bound in their coats, their trousers, their turbans, and their other garments, and were cast into the midst of the burning fiery furnace. ²²Therefore, because the king's command was urgent, and the furnace exceedingly hot, the flame of the fire killed those men who took up Shadrach, Meshach, and Abed-Nego. ²³And these three men, Shadrach, Meshach, and Abed-Nego, fell down bound into the midst of the burning fiery furnace.

The king sat comfortably in his seat waiting to hear the screams of these faithful rebels and see the smoke from their burning bodies rise in pillars into the sky. He could not help noticing that there was no smoke and not so much as a whimper. Then we read in vv. 24,25, "Then King Nebuchadnezzar was astonished; and he rose in haste and spoke, saying to his counselors, 'Did we not cast three men bound into the midst of the fire?' They answered and said to the king, 'True, O king.'" King Nebuchadnezzar then said, "Look! I see four men loose, walking in the midst of the fire; and they are not hurt, and the form of the fourth is like the Son of God." He might as well have said, "God of Israel, I know You are in there. Come out." He saw something that he had never seen before and the stand of these favored men made a believer out of him.

God allows difficulties in our daily walk so that He might stay present in our hearts and minds. His presence attracts Satan, and the angrier Satan gets, the bigger his fits become. But the greater the embarrassment to the enemy, the greater the glory to God and the magnitude of His miracles. The larger the trial is, the larger the magnitude of that miracle will be.

Martyred in the Holy Land

"I WANT YOU to be Muslim."

The man's voice cut through the bustle of the Palestine Bible Society's Christian bookstore in Gaza. It was 2007 and he was talking to bookstore manager Rami Ayed. The twenty-six-year-old Rami smiled sardonically. He was sure the man's assertion was a joke. Make him Muslim, are you kidding? There was no way he would convert to Islam. Yes, he lived in Gaza, the largest city in the Islam-dominated Palestinian territories. The idea of Christians living in Gaza—home to Hamas, the PLO, and much terrorism in the name of nationalism—was only as dangerous as the idea of Jews living in Gaza. Still, more than three thousand Christians lived there at the time of Rami's encounter at the bookstore.

"Okay, no problem," Rami said to the Muslim man. "I will be a Muslim for one month and you be a Christian for one month. I'll see if I like Islam and you see if you like Jesus."

The Muslim man vehemently shook his head. Rami did not understand his seriousness. So the man decided to emphasize his point.

"I know how to make you Muslim," he said threateningly as he walked out.

Rami was a dedicated Christian but he was not immune to Muslim threats. The Christian bookstore had been bombed twice —a pipe bomb had destroyed the doors in 2006 and a large bomb nearly destroyed the entire store in April 2007. There were threatening calls to his home. And he didn't know it, but he was being watched.

(continued)

(continued)

But even with all the on-site bullying, the death-threat phone calls, and the stalking, Rami never forgot his love for what he called "the poor people without Jesus." He even used part of his small salary from the bookstore to buy milk and diapers for Muslim children. "They are poor people and Jesus loves us all," he would say.

On October 7, 2007, Rami showed up at the Christian bookstore in the morning like always to open the store. He and the store employees ate breakfast together. His family had urged him to quit his job, saying it was too dangerous. But Rami refused. On that October day as Rami was closing up at 4 p.m., just like he did every day, someone came to talk to him. Two hours later he called his family telling them he would be late. Reportedly, he told his family he had been kidnapped and the kidnappers were trying to force him to convert to Islam. After a few hours his family called Rami back, but his phone was cut off mid ringtone: "Lord, You are my King and my Jesus..." *Click.*

It was 2 a.m. when the doctor called Rami's family. Rami was found in front of the Christian bookstore, his body riddled with bullets and stab wounds. His kidnappers had tried to make him Muslim and he refused to deny his Lord.

"We lost him," says Madeline, Rami's sister-in-law. "But he gained Jesus."

We can be just like Shadrach, Meshach, and Abed-Nego and boldly stand for our God. We must not hold back in sharing the message of grace available through a King named Jesus. I want to encourage you to find your identity within your relationship with the Father. Strengthen your weak points by preparing yourself daily and becoming a walking miracle. The possibilities that come out of standing firm in your convictions to the Scripture are beautiful.

It starts with you and spreads to the person next to you. Ask yourself who you are when it comes to God. Where do you stand when you're confronted with your faith? Do you see the importance of being a radical Christian, even if it comes at any cost? How will you react to confrontation when you are faced with it? What is the first thing that comes to mind when you think of making a difference for eternity? The more you question, the more your questions will be answered and the more your wisdom will be increased through God's Word. Search God's Word to find your true identity.

For we are His workmanship, created in Christ Jesus for good works, which God prepared beforehand that we should walk in them.

EPHESIANS 2:10

As the wicked are hurt by the best things, so the godly are bettered by the worst.

JOHN BUNYAN

CHAPTER 7

Bring It On

*Walk with a New Boldness
in Your Life*

THOSE WHO ARE considered to be radical Christians choose to continue teaching and sharing about what our Savior did on the cross. They choose to never turn down an opportunity to share Christ's message and to never back down from what they know is the scriptural truth. No matter what obstacles the enemy places in the road they continue to push forward, redeeming the time.

To face persecution and confrontation, just start by being different.

Don't Be Afraid to Be Different

Being different makes you stick out from the other humdrum people around you. In some areas of the world, being confrontational with your faith doesn't lead to stereotyping— meaning you can witness publicly or go to another country for a mission trip and no one would think anything of it. More and more, however, Christianity today is being attacked worldwide. Many Christians are confused about whether it is okay to say they are Christians for fear of the negative stereo-typing that comes with it.

Persecution is on the rise. In many areas in my country it is dangerous to go to church or carry a Bible, and Christians often cannot find employment because those in power tend to stand with their own. It is especially dangerous to be boldly faithful. There is no need for you and me to carry a Bible or wear a shirt with a verse or pass out tracts to be singled out or verbally attacked. Just walk down the street in many countries and you will see Satan defying God through movies, media, education, and entertainment. Even the church itself has become a place through which Satan works to strengthen his power against God.

The World's Money and Power Does Not Equal Justification

People on both sides of the Israeli-Palestinian conflict compare our ministry with wealthy organizations funded by the government or private organizations worldwide, or with big denominations that control much of the land and finances in Israel and the Palestinian territories. They believe the one with the most money and land is the one who controls things in the region. The thought is that if you have more power or money, you are more right and more justified than anyone else. But heaven cannot be bought with money. If it could, then the wealthy in the world would have bought it all out by now.

A while ago I visited a friend of mine named Daniel who was interning at a church in Florida. My wife and I decided to spend a few days with him and the youth he is working with. While on our trip down there, after spending the day out in the sun playing sports, the group got hungry and decided to go to Taco Bell for a quick bite. During the few days that we were with Daniel, I met a young man named John who I felt needed someone to stand by him. He was a quiet young man, but it was obvious to me that he had many secrets and scars buried deep in his heart.

My first day there I tried to talk to him and encourage him to lay all his burdens at the feet of Christ, and I told him that life was too short to carry burdens. "Let go and smile," I told him. "You were made to be a winner." John did not say much to me after that, but as we were loading the bus to go to Taco Bell, I noticed that John was standing all by himself. I got out of the bus and walked over to him to make sure he was coming with us. He said no, he would rather not because he had other plans. "Are you sure?" I asked. "We're just going for a quick bite. We'll be right back," I coaxed. With his face to the ground and his hands in his ripped pants pocket he replied, "No, thanks, I can't go."

Persecution is on the rise. In many areas in my country it is dangerous to go to church or carry a Bible, and Christians often cannot find employment... It is especially dangerous to be boldly faithful.

Now, I've lived long enough in the Middle East to read people, especially when they do not have enough money to join a group for dinner or an activity. I was not convinced that he didn't want to come, and being the good Middle Easterner that I am, I would not take no for an answer. I said, "John, you are coming with us and I am paying for your lunch." Shari, John, and I rode in the church bus with the group to Taco Bell for a quick lunch before Shari and I had to head out on the road again.

When we got to the restaurant I stared at the big white menu board, thinking of all the wonderful foods I could eat. We don't get a lot of Taco Bell in the West Bank. When I arrived at the front counter I weighed my options and, though I was really hungry and wanted more, I ordered several tacos and a soda. When I reached into my pocket, I realized that I had forgotten to bring in my wallet! I must have accidentally packed it somewhere in our luggage. I knew that we were in trouble.

It was pretty embarrassing because there was a long line of people waiting and watching as I fumbled around in my pockets. Shari pulled out a few dollar bills and some change from her purse. It wasn't really enough for three, so I asked Shari and John what they wanted and canceled my order. The total came to $8.45, the exact amount of money Shari had in her purse. I was so relieved. Poor Shari had been scraping around the inner lining of her purse to find every last penny.

I waited on the side while the two orders were being processed, which was very hard for me because I had to watch everyone grabbing their juicy steak fajitas and taking them back to their tables with glee. Smelling all the delicious food was the worst. As I waited, everyone who had ordered before me and after me got their meals and began eating, but we still did not have our order. So I waited a few more minutes before looking over at Shari to see what she wanted to do. My sweet wife gave me the Steve-I'm-dying-I-need-my-food-now look so I asked one of the managers if there was a problem with our order.

The manager looked at my receipt and apologized as she handed John and Shari their meals, saying, "Sir, there was a mixup on the order and we have extra food here that was prepared by mistake. If you would like to have it, feel free." My stomach urged me to take the tray so I thanked the manager and went to sit with the rest of the group. As I sat down I realized there were a couple of extra meals on the tray. There was the order that I originally intended to get plus two other items that I wanted but never told the cashier about. Clearly, God chose to make up for our financial lack.

I had a great time with John that day as we shared in God's blessings. Call it what you want, I look at all the little details and I like to see God's blessings over a cheerful giver. I do not boast in myself; I boast in the circumstances that Christ has allowed me to go through that make me who I am today. Matthew 6:26 says,

> "Look at the birds of the air, for they neither sow nor reap nor gather into barns; yet your heavenly Father feeds them. Are you not of more value than they?"

We do not need money or possessions to be recognized as legitimate or more "right" on certain issues, despite what the law of the land in my country seems to be. All I need is my Bible and the constant reminder of God's promises to us. Belonging to a rich organization or an institute with a large number of followers or a powerful denomination does not mean that you are right in what you believe. Instead, focus on being grounded in Christ, who cares nothing for the riches of man. The deeper in love with Christ we become, the wiser He will make us and the better we will be able to face confrontation and persecution.

Don't Be Embarrassed to Share Scripture

Representatives from The Voice of the Martyrs met with me once and we did a video interview about persecution and the current state of Christians in the region. A few months later I started to receive email threats, warning me to get the video off the Internet or something terrible would be done to me. Honestly, when I first saw those emails I thought they were sent to the wrong guy; I had forgotten all about the interview and didn't realize it had been posted online. I opened the link to the video and watched the three-minute interview where I talked about Christ being the only way to heaven and how we must love our enemies and forgive them.

In this instance, I was talking about the Jews and that God loves them just like He loves everyone else, and I added that He has a special love for the ones who follow the Messiah. I replied to one particular email where I felt the person attacking me was serious about his threats. I asked him what was wrong with what I said. "Tell me why you are so angry," I wrote. "I only spoke my heart and what I believe. This is the answer to today's problems and it's in God's Word if you do not believe me."

His reply was that I should not speak about everything that the Bible teaches. "You are the minority in what you believe," he wrote, "and what you are saying will cause much confusion in the minds and hearts of people." I replied back to him and asked him, "What if what I said will change many and affect lives to act differently, ending in an eternal peace, unconditional love, and joy in salvation?" He never wrote again and I am still alive, so maybe he heard something he was not used to. As Proverbs 15:1 says, "A soft answer turns away wrath."

A Courageous Christian Is a Noticed Christian

Truth causes doubt in the enemies' minds and hearts. In Daniel 3:24–26, we see a reaction from the world that is truly amazing.

24Then King Nebuchadnezzar was astonished; and he rose in haste and spoke, saying to his counselors, "Did we not cast three men bound into the midst of the fire?"

They answered and said to the king, "True, O king."

25"Look!" he answered, "I see four men loose, walking in the midst of the fire; and they are not hurt, and the form of the fourth is like the Son of God."

26Then Nebuchadnezzar went near the mouth of the burning fiery furnace and spoke, saying, "Shadrach,

Meshach, and Abed-Nego, servants of the Most High God, come out, and come here." Then Shadrach, Meshach, and Abed-Nego came from the midst of the fire."

All through the story in Daniel 3, we see amazement, confusion, and even anger caused by the surprises that King Nebuchadnezzar experienced. He had never witnessed such a complete rejection of diplomacy or such a strong belief in one God. Whenever the enemy testifies to the presence of God, you know that an even bigger miracle is coming.

Since when does the world rise up to greet something that God is doing, especially when His message comes through His faithful? Could we once again see nations rise up and become witnesses for the Father? I believe it is possible. I know it sounds overwhelming, but all it takes is to have full confidence in Christ's presence and remember that the Holy Spirit travels in the hearts of all believers wherever they go. Speak out, Christian, when confronted about your faith and share the simple truth that changed your life.

In v. 24 we see the enemy caused them to doubt themselves, but they began to question the power of the doubter and start to marvel at the power of Jehovah. You know you've got the enemy confused when he witnesses his own plot turning against him. That is exactly what happens when God's children stand up for the truth—they cause doubt in the hearts of the enemy, and with their living testimonies they can turn people to the Father. We are attractive Christians when we are courageous Christians. That is what we see happen in v. 27, as the king tells the three men to "come out, and come here":

And the satraps, administrators, governors, and the king's counselors gathered together, and they saw these men on whose bodies the fire had no power; the hair of their head was not singed nor were their garments affected, and the smell of fire was not on them.

Here the king and his servants are all gathered around, drawn to the powerful faith of the three Jewish men. They saw the evidence of God in their lives and wanted to be in the presence of these godly men. That is what being bold with your faith does: it draws people to your message.

You might read this and say, "Hey, I want to be in this fire; I want to draw people to Christ through my message. I want to experience this fire that causes people to question their lives according to the miracles they see and experience through my life and the lives of other faithful followers." Christ's message, however, comes with a price. Sometimes the price might be your life or the life of someone you love and hold dear to your heart.

Your Testimony Is Your Greatest Gift to Others

I would like to share with you the story of my Uncle George. George was my father's oldest brother and the type of man you would not want to meet in a dark alleyway. Uncle George was 6 foot and 350 pounds. He was built like a bear, but meaner. He hardly ever laughed and carried a lot of baggage throughout the years. Of course, what do you expect from a man who was shot several times while driving a taxi?

Uncle George drove us to school for many years, and if you were to add up all the words that Uncle George spoke to us during that time, I do not think they would fill a page. There was a presence that he carried with him and when you sat next to him or stood with him, you were afraid. It was as if there was a warning siren that blared "Leave me alone," to anyone within a half-mile radius of my uncle. Uncle George lived on the Mount of Olives and he was the only traditional Greek Orthodox Christian out of three families living there.

One summer, when I was about sixteen, my father was invited to go to a conference at the Sea of Galilee and he had the opportunity to invite some guests. He asked me if I would like to invite Uncle George to the conference. "Are you sure you want to do that?" I asked him. He said we must try, that maybe Christ could penetrate his life and change him.

That day I went with my father to my uncle's house, and as we parked and got out of the car my father told me to pray and see what happened. "Hopefully," he said, "your uncle will accept our invitation." My father knocked on the door and I could hear Uncle George's big slippers hit the floor at every step as he came closer to the door. I have never seen my father so nervous before. As Uncle George opened the door my father whispered, "Hello, George," as if a little child were facing the principal for being up to no good.

"Yeah, what do you need?" Uncle George asked. My father stuttered as he invited Uncle George to a three-day prayer conference at the Sea of Galilee. "I want you to join us," he asked. Silence set in as my father's eyes and Uncle George's eyes locked. Uncle George opened his mouth and asked, "Will there be free food?" My father said yes. "Will there be a swimming pool?" My father said yes again. Uncle George suddenly replied in a quiet voice, "Sure, I will go."

I remember on the bus ride to the conference there were empty seats all around him. He wanted to talk to no one and no one wanted to talk to him because they felt uninvited. Once we arrived, we found that the swimming pool was closed, so I couldn't wait to see what was going to happen between Uncle George and my dad. The three days of the conference were filled with prayer, singing, and worshiping the Lord. We prayed and sang almost twelve hours each day. I looked for my uncle for those three days but did not see him except during the meal times. I wondered where he was during the meetings and sessions and what he was thinking about all this, especially since he wasn't able to enjoy the swimming he had expressed such interest in.

The final day of the conference we had a time of prayer and singing, asking the Holy Spirit to continue to bless our lives as we went back to Jerusalem. You could feel the presence of the Lord in that place; joy, peace, and love filled every room. The last forty minutes before the conclusion of the conference I kept seeing a few heads at the front bouncing and jumping up and down with joy. I could not see over the people's heads because I was sitting in the back, but I could not help wanting to find out who was jumping at the front and what was going on.

So, being the curious young man that I am, I stepped into the middle of the aisle and slowly walked up toward the front. As I approached the front row I could not believe my eyes. Uncle George grabbed me by the hand and started jumping in the air. I did not know what was wrong with him. But for the first time ever in my life I saw Uncle George smile, and it was the joy of the Lord written all over his face that finally made me understand. I started jumping with him, at first because he had me by the hands and if I didn't jump too I was afraid they might be ripped off, but then I noticed my father jumping in the air right next to him.

Uncle George bent down and kissed my cheeks and told me, "Steve, Jesus changed my life! I am a new person—I have joy all through my feet!" I jumped and danced right there with Uncle George, with Dad on the other side of us. It is an experience I will never, ever forget to the day I die. If Uncle George can be changed, then anyone can be changed. On the bus ride back, there was hardly anybody at the front of the bus; most of us were all at the back sitting around Uncle George, hearing him tell his stories and the experiences that have held him down for years. Christ said in John 12:32, "And I, if I am lifted up from the earth, will draw all peoples to Myself."

Uncle George was never the same. All you had to do was look at his face to see the joy. I will never forget that evening —when we arrived in Jerusalem, as we got off the bus Uncle George said, "We need a church here in Jerusalem." A few months later my father and I asked Uncle George to help us start a new church, which we called Calvary Baptist Church, in an unreached area one mile from Calvary's cross. Uncle George was one of the main leaders with us. He stood at the front greeting people during the opening ceremony of our church building. The neighborhood and people in the area did not like the fact that a "Christian cult" church had just opened and we began to see immediate resistance.

Our church building was robbed a couple of times, our church vehicles were vandalized, and there were a couple of fires on the outside walls of the church. Thankfully, no one ever got hurt, but it was very close on several occasions.

I mentioned earlier that Uncle George lived on the Mount of Olives where he was the only Christian. He saw this as a beautiful opportunity and began to witness to everyone on the mountain. There were many radicals living there, but that did not stop him from sharing how King Jesus turned his life 180 degrees. One evening Uncle George was at home when a loud bang sounded at his front door. He opened the door to find his elderly neighbor out of breath, asking Uncle George to help him. Before Christ changed my uncle's life at that conference on the shores of the Sea of Galilee, he would have slammed the door in the man's face and told him he was busy. But now he was a changed man. Uncle George knew he had nothing to fear because heaven was on the other side of death's door. Seeing that his neighbor was very scared and worried, my uncle decided to invite him into his home. In our culture inviting someone into your home means that you are willing to stand with this person, even laying down your life for him.

As Uncle George stepped out into the courtyard, several men attacked him. He was beaten repeatedly with sharp-edged metal bars on his face and head, until he took his last breath. He left behind five children and a hurting, confused wife. He died at the front doorstep of his home, a martyr. His death caused a great revival in Jerusalem. People from all around the country and city heard about what happened to Uncle George. Even people from surrounding Arab countries and the U.S. heard of his courageous sacrifice. God used my uncle's death to give us an opportunity to share the message of love and forgiveness with the people of Israel and the Palestinian territories. I hold no grudge toward my uncle's killers. I hope and pray that they understand the love of Christ displayed on the cross and trust Him as their Savior.

I have learned that great things come at a greater cost. The Lord taught me that life is short and that even at death, He has a purpose for us.

I am not worried about Uncle George. He loved Jesus' words in Luke 17:33: "Whoever seeks to save his life will lose it, and whoever loses his life will preserve it." Nothing could stop Uncle George from laying down his life; in fact, I think that is how he would have wanted to die. He would not settle for less than a death that would save the life of others. I will never forget what the elderly neighbor testified at the funeral. He said, "George was never the same after that conference at the Sea of Galilee. Many people got really angry with him for witnessing about Jesus Christ, especially the radicals in the community. As they were beating him they yelled that this was the Christian man, he deserved it." Shortly afterward, the church that Uncle George envisioned and helped us start was shut down due to the pressure on the owner of the building and the radicals' resistance to our ministering in the community. I have learned that great things come at a greater cost. The Lord taught me that life is short and that even at death, He has a purpose for us.

Persecution Ignites Passion

This persecution and confrontation drew us close to Christ. To be in the fire that touches lives you must allow yourself to be used by God. We must practice being radical Christians by saying no to Satan's ways and yes to God's ways, igniting the fire in our lives. Toward the end of Daniel 3, King Nebuchadnezzar called for the "servants of the Most High God" to come out (v. 26). Amazed that they were unharmed, he blessed God and acknowledged "there is no other God who can deliver like this" (v. 29). It took much humility on the part of the king to publicly admit that the gods he worshiped were inferior to the one true God of Shadrach, Meshach, and Abed-Nego.

The first step to stand in the fire is to ignite that flame. To be ignited you must be willing to be confrontational with your faith, to stand strong and speak the truth of who Jesus Christ is. Since persecution and confrontation will face you sooner or later, be ready for it and enjoy the presence of God as you witness Him working through you.

As our persecution grew, so did our passion and love for Christ. These kinds of incidents also draw us closer to each other. Once our building was taken from us, we began to hold church meetings and private Bible studies to keep the spirit of growth and unity tangible in the lives of the believers and converts. New Testament churches grew through persecution and it seemed ours was doing the same. The stronger the attacks and persecution from the enemy, the more powerful the gospel message became. The death of Uncle George and loss of the church building ignited among our network of Christians a new vision and a new zeal to reach out to the same people in the same area where my uncle was killed. Bring it on.

I expect to pass through life but once.
If therefore, there be any kindness I can show,
Or any good thing I can do to any fellow being,
Let me do it now, as I shall not pass this way again.

WILLIAM PENN

But you have carefully followed my... persecutions,
afflictions, which happened to me at Antioch, at
Iconium, at Lystra—what persecutions I endured.
And out of them all the Lord delivered me.

2 TIMOTHY 3:10,11

CHAPTER 8

Against All Odds

Stories of Overcoming the Impossible

AFTER I FULLY accepted the new call to Jerusalem and began to work in the city, I noticed the spiritual thirst in the lives of the people. Starting a ministry for God was a challenge. Like most people, we face problems either from those closest to us or from the enemy himself—or both. It's interesting how God works things out. When Satan lifts up a human being, everything seems to be smooth and paved for the person, but when God's children begin to work all hell breaks loose, aimed at rocking our foundations and sending us back home.

As I began to do home visitations and would walk the streets where Uncle George walked, memories of his life and death would attempt to discourage me. Many times fear, doubt, and confusion would haunt every step I took to reach the same people group where my uncle was martyred and the Calvary Church building was taken from us and closed down. I was constantly confronted by earlier incidents that took place in my life to discourage God's mission in my life. I was told that I would not make it in Jerusalem because it is the most difficult place on earth, occupied by the three strongest people groups in the world, all fighting to be heard and to be the dominant one.

Since I tend to stutter and speak way too fast I was told that people would laugh at me, causing more damage to the work of Christ. I was labeled as an inexperienced, persistent boy who would make a mockery of himself and the gospel. I was also told that we cannot compete with other ministries because they have money and international clout as well as numbers, and we don't. No one thought that the ramifications of Uncle George's death and the persecution I went through could have an influence in igniting within me a consuming fire for Christ.

The Adversary at Work

I was impassioned with the desire to do something for Christ among the exact people who refused my uncle and our church. I had the blessings of the Lord, my heart was filled with a passion for Jerusalem, and I was fueled with excitement believing that I could see the impossible become possible. No one believed we could do it; many would discourage me as I chose to confront the enemy head on.

It is so amazing how strong Satan's presence is in the country of Israel and the Palestinian territories. As I was discussing my heart with a brother, he mentioned something very interesting about Jerusalem. He told me that Jerusalem's longitude and latitude added together equal 66.6.

I couldn't believe what he said so I went online to check it out. According to www.timeanddate.com, the center of the city of Jerusalem is 31° 47' N by 35° 13' E. If we add the numbers together we get 66° 60' (or 66.6). This of course may simply be a coincidence, but the probability of this happening could be a million to one. Although I am not a superstitious person, I still do not like that number and never will.

I never thought that starting a work would be as difficult as it was in Jerusalem, especially after coming from the U.S. where everyone is free to share their religion. Bethlehem was difficult, but we are finding Jerusalem even more so. As my father and I, along with Uncle George and others, began Calvary Baptist Church in Jerusalem, I remember asking God what He would have me do and in what part of Jerusalem I should begin His work. I spent time fasting and praying on my knees, asking God to share His plans for Jerusalem with me.

Christians are in the minority in Israel, especially those ministering to the people of the surrounding areas. I searched for a place to begin ministering but nothing opened up. I asked God, "Who will rent us a place to use as a ministry to reach people with the gospel?" I remember meeting with landlords. We would wrap up all the details and agreements, but when it came down to what we would be using the building for, everything suddenly flew out the window. The fear of what radicals would do to the landlord or their properties was a real concern.

After searching for months with no opened doors, I was tired and ready to quit searching. "Lord," I prayed, "I'm done looking. I need you to step in and get us the right place." The next day my father took me with him to pray a blessing on a new building a man had just constructed for his business. When we arrived the owner showed us around as my father blessed every room. When we got to the basement my father prayed, "Lord, I ask that you bless this man and all his work. I ask that this building would be used to glorify your name. Amen." After my father finished praying the man turned to me and asked, "Aren't you looking for a church building?"

I had never told this man anything about a church and it's not like the other landlords I had visited would want to talk about it. I was so stunned, I stood frozen and speechless for a few seconds. Stuttering, I finally said yes, I was, and he informed me I could rent his basement floor if I hadn't already said yes to someone else. I could not help my eyes tearing up as I began to walk around, imagining people raising their hands, some clapping or kneeling at the front altar asking Christ to save them and turn their lives around.

Overcoming Obstacles in Daily Life

We shook hands and the next day I signed a contract and moved in. This was the second building that Calvary had occupied due to pressures and persecution, but soon we started to see many doors open up. The need for a ministry in the area was very evident. We began our meetings as always, accepting every person who came through our doors no matter their ethnicity, gender, or nationality. People heard something in our teaching that they did not hear anywhere else. They were shocked to hear teaching about God's love and forgiveness. They were amazed at the fact that a man they did not know would die on the cross for their sakes two thousand years ago. They were shocked to see that Messianic Jewish believers and Western Christians would reach out to an Arab Christian church as unified brothers in Christ. Many were also shocked that we were able to establish a church and keep its doors open in a very hostile, difficult area.

The neighborhood kids began to be affected and they drew in kids to our programs and activities. Unfortunately, our ministry affected others, too. We started to see neighbors get mad at what the children were learning and taking home. Resistance came from neighbors saying we were not teaching truth and that the noise was too loud. The police were called on us for having an overcrowded building and cars blocking the roads. I probably would have wound up in jail if the police captain hadn't been willing for me to show him around and explain exactly what we were doing and how we functioned.

He was so touched and amazed he told us to continue our work and that we'd be safe.

As we started to outgrow our church building, Satan took opportunity after opportunity to escalate confrontations and attacks. The church sign was torn down, shredded to pieces, and laid at the front entrance of the church doors. The building was targeted by vandals and robberies became a weekly reality. Our good-hearted landlord was being robbed because of our church. We didn't want to continue to bring him hardship so we decided it was time to move and find a bigger building. We found a temporary building but were asked to leave when the front doors of the church were ripped off their hinges by aggressors. Again, all the landlords' hearts were hardened against our ministry. We went out looking for our third building, knocking on doors, seeking God's plan.

Despite the resistance from persecutors, many people came to us with that need to be loved and accepted. This is a universal need, but I feel that the people here in Israel have a special desire for love—and we all have a need for God's forgiveness in Christ. We've finally found a temporary church building, but I do not believe it will be for long.

The harvest is plenty here, but the workers are few because we struggle to keep our faithful brothers and sisters alive. Due to the enemy's victories—through martyrdom, death threats, believers fleeing, unemployment, and much more—we are growing weaker as our numbers and outreaches decline. One troubling statistic is that in the year 2000, more than 10,000 Christian families left Bethlehem, Jerusalem, and the surrounding cities. According to the Israeli Ministry of Christian affairs, out of 7.8 million people there are fewer than 20,000 evangelicals in the Israeli and Palestinian territories. I have been in churches in the U.S. where there are more members in that one church than there are in our entire country.

Another problem is that Israel is closed to missions. By law foreigners are prohibited from coming to serve as missionaries or to proselytize. Because of a fear of new ministries being established, foreigners are being pushed out of the country by the Israeli government with the excuse that Christian visitors have overstayed their welcome. When their visas expire they are not being extended. Recently, many foreign missionaries have been coming in either under a school or work visa, both of which are limited to four or five years.

Facing the Impossible Task

It is crazy to think that in the place where our faith began such a spirit of hatred, killing, violence, and persecution can exist. That this is the place where the cross stood and where Christ defeated Satan is truly unbelievable. The reality is that the small minority of Christians remaining in the region are still carrying the flag. We must see Christians worldwide start to extend the hand of friendship and care to the Israeli and Palestinian peoples.

> It is crazy to think that in the place where our faith began such a spirit of hatred, killing, violence, and persecution can exist. That this is the place where the cross stood and where Christ defeated Satan is truly unbelievable.

Since the challenge is great and Israel is closed to foreigners, opportunity is offered through locals like us to promote the gospel of Jesus Christ. We have an obligation to stand up and make a difference. I count it a blessing that God would consider using a stuttering young Palestinian like me. I am honored to say that I have had the opportunity to aid in God's work in this land. Our influence reaches beyond people in the street. We have seen God bring my father and I into the paths of influential leaders like King Hussein of Jordan and his son King Abdullah, Israeli leaders like President Shimon Peres, President Moshe Katsav and Prime Minister Netanyahu, PLO Chairman Abu Mazen, and many others.

Meeting these influential people I could do nothing more than tell them, "I am praying for you and your country," or "I am asking the Lord to be with you." Most leaders would look into my eyes as they shook my hands tightly and say thank you, though there were those times I would get the look of confusion or dismissal.

How do we keep strong? We keep strong by remembering the love of Jesus Christ and knowing that He has had a hand on our work. I have been there; I have seen God work and I have heard His voice. In the case of Shadrach, Meshach, and Abed-Nego, we read that "the satraps, administrators, governors, and the king's counselors gathered together, and they saw these men on whose bodies the fire had no power..." (Daniel 3:27). First the attention was on the three radical believers, but then the spotlight shifted to critique the king and the witnesses who saw the whole incident and were "astonished" (v. 24). When we as Christians are willing to be used by God, He will be willing to use us. People will respond effectively to the boldness of that kind of witness. We must all be a walking testimony wherever we go, especially when we are asked about our faith directly. Do not rob a seeker of a blessing; share the gospel throughout your life.

> *We must all be a walking testimony wherever we go, especially when we are asked about our faith directly. Do not rob a seeker of a blessing; share the gospel throughout your life.*

Through our faithful witness, Jews, Muslims, atheists, and others across the globe could one day be turned around to declare that Jesus Christ is the King of kings and Lord of lords. Philippians 2:10,11 says,

> ...that at the name of Jesus every knee should bow, of those in heaven, and of those on earth, and of those under the earth, and that every tongue should confess that Jesus Christ is Lord, to the glory of God the Father.

Christians today can take a simple step of faith by refusing to be diplomatic Christians and by standing up for what they believe. We must grow in faith with God before we can be sent into the world by God.

Overcoming Death

Before I left Bethlehem to go to college in the U.S., every year we would host a Vacation Bible School. VBS is a time for children to be challenged by hearing new life-changing Bible stories, playing games, learning new Bible songs and the movements that go with them, as well as creative arts and crafts that let them express their love for Christ in their own unique ways. The kids get to do what kids do and enjoy time away from violence, shooting, and hatred.

This is one of the reasons we hold these camps, to try to plant the message of love, forgiveness, peace, and joy in whatever short time we have them for. Vacation Bible School gives us the unique opportunity to show these kids love early on and expose them to forgiveness by explaining Christ's message from the cross.

These kids are always all over the place. The first day the kids always test their boundaries. When I walk into the sanctuary I usually find kids hanging on the ceiling fans, out the window, or halfway inside the speakers. They come from all backgrounds, religions, towns, and cities. They arrive expecting to take home the usual candy, food, clothing, toys, and other items that we pass out to them every year, but they go home with a lot more. On top of these things, they go home with a Bible in Arabic and the message of Christ's life on videotape. These things are provided through the sacrificial giving of involved Christians who understand the importance of children's ministries.

I will never forget the summer of 2000 Vacation Bible School. That year we had more kids than ever—our record number of 290 kids ranging from ages 5 to 15. That summer we saw the Lord touch the lives of many young people. The Holy Spirit worked in the life of one particular young girl in our youth group. Her name was Lina and she came from a very tough home.

The first time she walked through our church doors we could tell that she was heavily burdened. She lacked a love for life because she never experienced true love and compassion. I noticed that every time Lina came to church she would cry and most of the time walk out. So after watching her for several weeks I invited her to come to our youth group. She began to cry again, so I stopped her outside by the thick steel doors of our front entrance and I said, "Lina, Christ loves you and He will forgive your sins and give you joy and peace if you ask Him. I would like you to come and be with us in our youth meeting on Saturday. We want you to know we love you." She did not say a word, just looked up from the floor, shook her head in confusion, and walked out.

The next week Lina came back to the youth meeting crying. I asked her what was wrong, but she said she did not know. I asked her again, "Lina, what is wrong?" Again she replied, "I do not know." I asked her how she felt and she replied with a question: "Why is it that every time I enter your church building I feel a weight being lifted off my chest, and I forget everything that is hurting in my life? Why do I need to cry here?" I explained that it was God drawing her. I told her she could not see Him, but Christ through the Holy Spirit was calling her to repent and surrender to Him. At that moment Lina prayed and placed her trust in Jesus as the risen Christ, making Him number one in her life.

Lina's journey had begun. She went from a sad and hurting soul to a happy, joyful person filled with love and compassion. I wish I could draw a picture of her before and after Christ just to give you a glimpse of the joy in her life. Her parents visited us occasionally, and one time they came to meet with us to ask what had happened to their daughter. They said, "She is so different—she has hope, and is happy and smiling. We want that same joy and peace in our lives." So we shared the gospel with them, explaining how Christ can forgive their sins and give them eternal life. Right there on the church entrance Lina's mother and father repented of their sins and trusted in Christ as their personal Savior.

Lina did not believe in keeping the joy of Christ to herself, so she made sure to share it with anyone and everyone who crossed her path. That particular summer of 2000 Lina came up to me and asked if she could invite a few more kids from her neighborhood. I could not turn her down. You wouldn't either if you saw her excitement and zeal to reach kids for Christ. That summer she invited two full vanloads of kids. By the end of the week these kids heard about why Jesus Christ died and how they could meet Him and know Him personally. Not only did we have the largest number ever in attendance, but that last day we had the largest number of children walk up to the front to pray and ask to know who Jesus was because they wanted Him in their lives. Kids were pouring down the aisles from all over the big meeting hall. We ran out of space in the front so we had them in the corners and on the sides, being taught how to receive Christ and to understand the Holy Spirit's presence in their lives. These children took home more than just presents, they took home Jesus Christ's love and joy. Every child that day infiltrated their homes with the greatest treasure ever.

That summer before I left for the U.S., I was asked to speak and give a message. I chose to speak about the promises that Christ has for us in heaven and the consequences when we refuse to accept Jesus Christ. That Sunday evening Lina was there and she invited her older sister to come with her. They were both sitting at the back left corner of the church hall. They were listening, especially her older sister who attentively followed every word of the message.

At the end of the message I told people that heaven is near, and that we can take part in the promises that Christ gave us. I also told the people sitting there that Jesus Christ came to give us life and joy. "It is simple," I told them. "All we have to do is to trust in Jesus Christ and ask Him to become the Lord of our lives." As an Arabic song entitled "I Have Victory in the Blood of Christ" began to play, Lina's older sister stood up crying. I walked to the back and prayed with Lina's sister. She kept repeating the phrase, "Jesus, give me joy, please," over and over again. She repeated this plea as tears flowed down her face. If you walked into that place that night, you would have felt heaven in Bethlehem.

Months later I began my journey in the U.S. at school, and at four o'clock one morning the phone rang and I didn't pick it up, thinking it was a wrong number. It persisted to ring again and again so slowly I got up, tripping over things on the floor, trying to pick up the phone in the dark. "Hello, Steven?" It was my father on the end of the line. There was something peculiar in the way he said my name.

I remember him asking, "Steven, are you up? I need you to sit up and lift your head up high. Steven, Lina and her older sister were both shot today. Their mother walked into their bedroom and found them both shot to death bleeding on the floor. The Bible that Lina kept on her nightstand was on the floor next to her." I could not hold it all in, and began to cry like I never had before. A feeling of emptiness and confusion came over me. I could not sleep for two days. I cried at the thought of Lina's loss and the joyful spirit she possessed.

What did she do to earn a bullet to the head? She confronted people with truth, and that truth is Jesus Christ. Lina's life changed by hearing the truth, so the truth was what she wanted for others.

Eventually the Holy Spirit began to show me through Scripture the joy in dying for Christ and how there is a place prepared for each and every one of us at an appointed time. Christ showed me how to turn tears of sadness into tears of joy. I wanted to cry and as I was crying I began to laugh and rejoice. As I dozed off I saw the entrance to heaven and at the front gates there were two forms of light standing and guarding the narrow entrance. There were Lina and her older sister, asking to see the King.

The guard told Lina and her sister to wait and in my dream I remember screaming at the angel, telling him, "Don't you know who these girls are?! They are Christ's martyred saints!" The King was called to the front gate and informed that there were two sinners waiting at the front. He walked toward the front gate and saw Lina and her sister standing there. The King looked at them and told the angels that they were not sinners but His daughters and that He wanted to walk out and let them in Himself. The King opened the gates and reached out to them both, holding their hands tightly as He walked them both into His Kingdom. I do not know if that is exactly what happened, but I thank God for the peace He gave me in that dream and for the knowledge I possess of both girls' salvation.

We found out later that Lina was being harassed by many radicals in the community for taking their children to VBS and exposing them to Jesus Christ. This act of violence was a sign to everyone to watch out for their lives if they were witnessing about Jesus Christ.

When I think of what those men did I ask, "What horrible act did Lina commit to make her worthy of death? What did she do to earn a bullet to the head?" She confronted people with truth, and that truth is Jesus Christ. Lina's life changed by hearing the truth, so the truth was what she wanted for others. She did not want anyone to be robbed of the joy offered by Jesus Christ. Even today the police won't touch their murder cases. Their deaths influenced the lives of many people of all ages, from all religions. It drew many to be confronted with the truth and reality of who Jesus is. What would Lina and her sister ask you and me to do differently? I believe they would tell us, *"Sharing Christ's joy is worth dying a thousand deaths."*

Standing Firm Results in Victory

At the conclusion of our passage in Daniel 3, King Nebuchadnezzar begins to boast at the magnificence of the power of the God of Israel.

> 28Nebuchadnezzar spoke, saying, "Blessed be the God of Shadrach, Meshach, and Abed-Nego, who sent His Angel and delivered His servants who trusted in Him, and they

have frustrated the king's word, and yielded their bodies, that they should not serve nor worship any god except their own God! [29]Therefore I make a decree that any people, nation, or language which speaks anything amiss against the God of Shadrach, Meshach, and Abed-Nego shall be cut in pieces, and their houses shall be made an ash heap; because there is no other God who can deliver like this."

In v. 28 we see the king testify publicly to the power of God and the extent of care and provision he saw in the work of the Lord. We continue in v. 29 to see the outcome of overcoming: once the enemy realizes God's servants would rather die than betray Him, he flees, and the confrontation between the king and the men of God results in supernatural occurrences. This is typical in the life of martyrs, whether they are from historic times or the present. We see that through the killing of a saint revival often breaks out and more lives are changed. The enemy knows a strong Christian when he sees our decision to act against him.

> *The same truth that changed your life and mine must be heard in your city and in Jerusalem and the West Bank. After all, it is not my Jerusalem, it is our Jerusalem.*

One Last Call

What has happened in our region in the Middle East is coming your way. The sooner you realize it, the faster you can start preparing to deal with it. We have read many testimonies of real-life people in our region today who have lost their lives for standing up and not being diplomatic. We also read in the life of Shadrach, Meshach, and Abed-Nego that the three faithful Jewish men were willing to be martyred for their testimony, and although they came close to death, God saved them. We can learn from their story how the enemy is always defeated, though he tries to make us forget that. We must conduct ourselves with honor and pride in the One who did it all for us on the cross. I hope and pray that you see the reality of persecution and confrontation in your hometown.

Remember every step of the way that we have already won the battle through Jesus Christ, so proclaim it every time you are asked and every time you are confronted. Let others in on what you know. I hope this book has awakened you to something I have seen happening, especially in the West. The influence of fundamental Islam is growing in America as in other places, and I hope you do not let the past repeat itself. You must understand something about the enemy, who uses those who seek to tear us down. Once he takes a little, he wants more, and once he takes more, he won't stop taking. This goes for your rights, your family values, your freedom, and your way of living. I pray that the Lord would give you the strength to stand up and the insight to see the fruit that comes out of being faithful. The same truth that changed your life and mine must be heard in your city and in Jerusalem and the West Bank. After all, it is not my Jerusalem, it is our Jerusalem.

Conclusion

To walk in the path of faith we must be willing to say yes to Christ and stand up. Once we say yes by faith we can face our enemy. As Christians we all have an obligation toward Israel's spiritual and physical state. The enemy of both the spiritual realm and the physical realm is getting stronger and stronger. I am constantly witnessing people physically and spiritually hurting, hungry, and searching for truth. We in Israel cannot do it alone; we need your help to continue making a difference.

Let's take back what is rightfully God's: the souls of His creation. Few Christians can come to Israel to live or start a ministry, but we have been here and will remain in this country until the Lord takes us home. We need the backing up of your prayers and spiritual and financial support to be able to continue changing lives and making a difference. Paul teaches us in 1 Corinthians 3:10,11:

> According to the grace of God which was given to me, as a wise master builder I have laid the foundation, and another builds on it. But let each one take heed how he builds on it. For no other foundation can anyone lay than that which is laid, which is Jesus Christ.

Paul knew that we all have a part in building the Kingdom and our duties comes in different shapes and sizes. You and I have the incredible privilege to know Christ, and with that knowledge comes responsibility. My prayer for you is this:

> Lord, I ask that You give wisdom and strength to these readers to understand Your ways and to see Your blessings. Lord, I ask that You would touch the readers to stand up for You, and that You give them understanding and discernment in confrontation. Lastly, Lord, I ask that You burden the hearts and minds of readers to take it upon themselves to pray for the peace of Jerusalem and give them the joy of participating in giving Your holiest land back to its rightful King.

I would like to hear from you and how the insights and stories in this book influenced you. Your words of love and encouragement mean a lot to all of our workers, church members, families, and especially to me. We love to hear how our brothers and sisters across the seas are growing, so please take the time to send us a quick email (info@holylandmissions.org) with your testimony, stories of blessings, or letters testifying to God's miracles in your life.

Epilogue

In 1990, I began to understand more about what was going on around me. My father told me, "Steven, the world is filled with evil and darkness. When hopelessness and despair surround you, look to this Book for a sign of God's promises to you." He handed me my first Bible ever, which was in the Arabic language. On the front page of my Bible was my father's letter to me. I would like to share it with you to invite you even deeper into my life and the ministries in which I serve.

> *January 6, 1990*
>
> *I give this Bible to my beloved dear son, Steven, so that it might be his motto, that this Bible is the best means to refresh one's spiritual life. I beg that you take care of it, and grow in it, so that the Lord might bless your life to be a loyal servant for Him.*
>
> *Your loving father,*
>
> *Naim B. Khoury*

I want to ask you to boldly partner with us, first in praying by asking the Lord to give all of our ministries wisdom and strength to deal with persecution and confrontation. Second, we ask you to plead for our people's protection and for the safety of our children and church workers, but especially from our enemies. Third, please pray for the Lord to provide the funds to purchase land and build a building, opening a door for our ministry in Jerusalem to reach more people.

We thank the Lord for the opportunities He has given us to serve in six ministries in both the Arab and Israeli territories all over the region. Satan has been trying to shut us down since 1979, and is daily trying to discourage us. Since July 2004, Satan has targeted our newest ministry, Calvary. Every day as I wake up to face the city of Jerusalem and its lost people, I cannot help but wonder: Will we be without a building today? Will I live to see another day?

When you read about our nation in the Bible or hear about it in the news, I would like to give you a brief explanation of our six ministries to help you understand each one and to help you pray better.

First, the Bethlehem Church, founded by my father, is based in the city of Bethlehem. We hold Bible studies, music outreaches, children's programs, youth programs, and weekly discipleship programs. Two to four hundred people go through our doors on a weekly basis. We estimate that since 1978, more than fifty thousand have professed Christ as their personal Savior.

Second, we have a church in Jericho, called Jericho Bible Church, located in the oldest city and lowest spot in the world. This ministry has affected the lives of many Muslims and local believers. Some of the key leaders in the Muslim community have been saved and affected by the Lord's work in Jericho. Many know our Jericho church as the last stop before the Jordanian border.

The Lord has also opened the door for us to establish the first and only evangelical Christian youth center in the town of Shepherds' Field. The doors are open to all to come in and enjoy an atmosphere that provides calmness, safety, and a spiritual safe haven. Every Friday the youth meet for a Bible study to discuss Christ's teachings. Through this simple place, hundreds have heard the message of Christ.

From the results of our Bible College, a brother was called to go back to his hometown of North Zababdeh and start a home church. So through that we are seeing many, especially from a traditional Christian background, follow Christ. Considering the history of this town's political turmoil, its people seek refuge in the hope that Christ gives.

Our fifth ministry is the Old City Jerusalem Church. My father and I had the vision to revive the Old City section called Ja-bsha right in the area of the Via Dolorosa, the road where Christ carried the cross. Its doors are open to the many living in the Old City of Jerusalem. The weekly meetings and outreaches of this Old City Church have touched many hearts, especially of those older in age.

Last but not least is our East Jerusalem church. This is our most recently established church, but not our last, Lord willing. Called Calvary Baptist Church, it is the continuing work and vision of my father and Uncle George. I chose to keep this name to remind me, every time persecution arises or Satan isn't going easy on us, that people and situations change. I was challenged to restart Calvary in July 2011, and it has been one of my greatest challenges. The area in East Jerusalem includes the cities Beit Hanina and Shuafat, both known for the fundamental extremist teaching and mindset. I believe the Lord has me there for a great purpose, even though it is very difficult. At Calvary we focus on outreaches like giving out the message of Christ through teaching music, sports, arts, and extracurricular activities. We have seen great and amazing miracles happen in people's lives and in this community.

As I am daily thinking about growing and expanding our outreach areas, God has laid it on my heart to build the first multipurpose worship center in Northeast Jerusalem. Such a work would show commitment to the local people. I recently was told that many look upon our churches, especially Calvary in East Jerusalem, as a safe haven from the world, a place to come to and learn about the love of Christ manifested on the cross, through the teaching of His Word.

We know that there will come a day when no one will offer us a place in which to worship, a day when even homes will no longer be safe places for believers to worship in secret. We know that the church is a body of believers and that to be a witness the body of Christ must reveal the work of Christ for others to see and experience. Since Christianity is a legal faith in Israel, we believe that there is a vital need for a multi-purpose outreach center for all to see and enter. Against all odds, even though everyone told me that we could not get a building license from the Israeli government or the support of the local community, we have an initial green light to begin the process. I still keep going with just my faith until the Lord provides the required funds to make it a reality. Through the testimonies and changed lives that I have seen, the Lord showed me the desperate need to build a stronger bridge between us and the locals in all of Jerusalem and the surrounding villages.

We know that there will come a day when no one will offer us a place in which to worship, a day when even homes will no longer be safe places for believers to worship in secret.

I saw the hunger on the hearts of the Arabs and Israelis when we began to hold music school programs to see how the locals would respond, and before we could advertise for the three-month music course it was completely booked! Young people would come through our doors thinking it would be only a music class, but sharing the love and passion of Christ for three months always pays off. By the end of every three-month course they would walk out knowing Christian songs, understanding who Jesus Christ is, and learning to love others.

So to further test the extent of the hunger and thirst of the people, we began a women's character course. We would invite women from the community and introduce them to what we are doing and what has touched our lives—Jesus Christ. We are weekly seeing Christ turn many lives around. "Why are they coming?" a person once asked me. I told him it was because we invite them in and show them love, so in return they feel safe and trust us.

Currently, we have seen so much resistance in the place we are renting. I honestly do not know how much longer we can remain there. So the urgency to do something is now more than ever on my heart. Our goal is to plant a multipurpose building.

Who do we go to for help? What doors do we knock on? We are going to God and asking Him to connect us with partners who would stand up and see the blessings of the Kingdom. How much are we investing and doing that is making a difference in heaven?

Go ahead and make a difference—join with us to make a difference in Jerusalem.

PASTOR STEVEN KHOURY

Questions for Reflection

1. In my life today, in what ways am I being a diplomatic Christian?

2. How is my faith being confronted, and by what means am I and the Christians around me being persecuted?

3. What aspect of my Christianity needs growth in order to equip me to face tomorrow's persecution?

4. How will I handle persecution when it comes my way?

5. Find three examples in the Bible where God allowed persecution to affect the lives of believers, and note how their
   lives were changed afterward.

The Persecuted Church

THE VOICE OF THE MARTYRS has many other books, videos, brochures, and other products to help you learn more about the persecuted church. In the U.S., to order materials or to receive our free monthly newsletter, call (800) 747-0085 or write to:

The Voice of the Martyrs
P. O. Box 443
Bartlesville, OK 74005-0443
www.persecution.com
thevoice@vom-usa.org

If you are in Canada, England, Australia, New Zealand, or South Africa, contact:

Australia:

The Voice of the Martyrs
P.O. Box 250
Lawson NSW 2783
Australia

Website: www.persecution.com.au
Email: thevoice@persecution.com.au

Canada:

The Voice of the Martyrs
P.O. Box 608
Streetsville, Ontario L5M 2C1
Canada

Website: www.persecution.net
Email: thevoice@vomcanada.org

New Zealand:
The Voice of the Martyrs
P.O. Box 5482
Papanui, Christchurch 8542
New Zealand

Website: www.persecution.co.nz
Email: thevoice@persecution.co.nz

South Africa:
Christian Mission International
P.O. Box 7157
1417 Primrose Hill
South Africa

Email: cmi@icon.co.za

United Kingdom:
Release International
P.O. Box 54
Orpington BR5 9RT
United Kingdom

Website: www.releaseinternational.org
Email: info@releaseinternational.org